D1631180

Testimonials for *Mud, Blood and Studs*

'We all have family histories, but not many can lay claim to the sporting history of the Brown family. Whether the shape of the ball is round or oval, or the team is Manchester United or British & Irish Lions, James Brown takes us on a journey where the ball's bounce takes us across the globe and the generations. There's even a third-place finish at the inaugural World Cup, the best-ever finish for the US men's national team. First and foremost, James is a top-notch researcher and an able writer, but he is also a son, grandson, brother, and father. He has a reverence and respect for his ancestors as he covers mid-century international sport, an era when those who played did so for the love of the game. Specifically, this book is about an important American soccer family, one who helped keep the flame of the sport alive during its "dark ages". As a driving force behind the Society for American History, James Brown has also brought light to our nation's soccer story. His family's story is our story.'

Tom McCabe, president, Society for American Soccer History

'The Brown legacy is the perfect example of the pioneering influence Scotland had on the world of soccer and rugby. This book provides exceptional first-hand insight into the world of the Scotch Professors, where home and abroad they took their ball, whether spherical or oval, and demonstrated their natural abilities and gifts to the communities they found themselves in, and in this family's case, on three separate continents. The Brown family, over many generations, became sporting legends both domestically and on the international stage, with their desire to excel in their sporting field born out of necessity. This compelling story shows their rise to the pinnacle of sporting achievement, and I commend the Brown family as one of the best examples of the Scotch Professors in sporting history.'

Graeme Brown, founder of the Hampden Collection

'As a journalist, researcher, and developer of many initiatives regarding soccer history that I am, it was just a matter of time for me to get in contact with James Brown and his passionate labour about his grandfather in the 1930 World Cup. Long expected by me and many others, this book is also a confirmation of something I always say, firmly believe and confirm almost every day: there's a lot of new things we can discover and do about the past in order to enrich and correct the way it was usually exposed. Yes: those old days can still be a source of new stories and revelations that can lead not only to a more accurate knowledge and understanding of those times and the people who lived back then, but also to such great fun and touching personal experiences. That is all contained in the story of James's ancestors, which is also the story of how sport developed in the USA, Scotland, and other parts of the world. A magnificent journey, which any football or rugby lover could not resist.'

Esteban Bekerman, founding director of Entre Tiempos

'Any football club with a long history will have players remembered long after they have hung up their boots. Old men and women will gather and recall those happy days of their youth when legendary players trod the turf of their favourite club. It's 100 years since the formation of Guildford City Football Club. Since 1921 there have been perhaps four or five players who truly could be considered "a legend" of the club. But arguably at the top of that list is Jim Brown. There will be very few people today who saw Jim play in the red and white stripes. Jim Brown was a goalscorer supreme and his period at the club between 1937 and 1940 coincided with Guildford's best ever side; a team that had World War Two not intervened may well have been elected to the Football League. Jim Brown made 150 appearances for Guildford City, scoring with his pace and shooting ability an incredible 148 goals. But there was far more to the man than three years spent in Guildford. Any man who scores in a World Cup semi-final, signs for Manchester United while on a transatlantic liner, and plays a part in the formation of the Players' Union is worthy of high acclaim.'

Barry Underwood MBE, secretary of Guildford City Football Club

'History tells stories and the best kind of stories are true ones with real characters and intriguing narratives. In *Mud, Blood and Studs*, James Brown shares much more than his own family history. He has painstakingly researched the life of the Brown booters (and Lambie and Brown ruggers) from Scotland to America, Mexico to South Africa, with a passion unique to family history. Following James's research journey these last few years has been a privilege and sharing in his discoveries a joy. How he has been able to build his own family football archive with unique material and sources from multiple continents should serve as a template for more of this kind of essential research into the sporting past. Whether it was how the matches "waxed hot", the fear of "razzberries" or even the "sentimental playing field", James has woven in the sporting details of universal human experience that make a personal story accessible to all.'

Dr Kevin Tallec Marston, research fellow and academic project manager for Centre International d'Etude du Sport, and member of the Society for American Soccer History

MUD, BLOOD AND STUDS

James Brown

MUD, BLOOD AND STUDS

One Family's Legacy in Soccer and Rugby
Across Three Continents

First published by Pitch Publishing, 2022

Pitch Publishing
9 Donnington Park,
85 Birdham Road,
Chichester,
West Sussex,
PO20 7AJ
www.pitchpublishing.co.uk
info@pitchpublishing.co.uk

A CIP catalogue record is available for this book from the British Library.

ISBN 978-1-80150-161-3

Typesetting and origination by Pitch Publishing

Printed and bound in Great Britain by TJ Books, Padstow

Contents

Foreword by George Brown

THE AUTHOR of *Mud, Blood and Studs*, James Cormack Brown, is my son and I am honoured that he has asked me to write the foreword.

This book is clearly a labour of love. It is the product of six years of dedicated research during which the author sifted through countless newspaper archives, both foreign and domestic, and boxes of family photographs well as conducting wide-ranging interviews with club historians, memorabilia collectors, family members, players and coaches.

It is richly illustrated with reams of photographs, many of which came from the private collections of those mentioned in the book as well as those of family members.

The narrative begins in 1927 when my father James Brown emigrated to the USA and follows his footballing career through the 1930 World Cup (where the USA finished third) and his stints with Manchester United, Tottenham Hotspur, and other prominent clubs. He is a member of the US Soccer Hall of Fame.

This book is peppered with insightful and revealing anecdotes. Of particular interest is his coverage of the rugby side of the family; both Scotland's Browns, Peter and Gordon, who were capped for Scotland, as well as the Lambie side of the family which emigrated to South Africa. Patrick Lambie was capped 60 times for South Africa.

Mud, Blood and Studs provides a rare insight into the football and rugby careers of a talented sporting clan and the author is to be complimented for his objectivity and the depth of his research. It is a damn good read.

Introduction

AT ONE point or another in your life – whether through work, friendships, or eventual relationships – the question about your family origins comes up. Most often, you mention your parents and where they are from. Or you might talk about your grandparents, especially if they came from another country, or discuss where you've lived and how come. But when you grow up in a sporting family who came from very little, you tend to look at life and the future in a different light. No matter what sport or how big or small it may be, there are always fascinating stories to be told and to be passed along to the next generations; that's exactly what this book was meant to be.

Six long years ago, I took up the task of exploring, researching and documenting the paternal Brown side of the family because I was fascinated by the rich mixture of stories about the football (soccer) and rugby careers of family members from Scotland to South Africa through the Lambie branch of the family.

This book was initially intended for my son, so that he would have a comprehensive look at his US/UK side of the family, since we live in the Paris region and he hadn't had the chance to visit the US or UK at that point. I always mentioned them – but it's not the same as reading, seeing photos, and physically walking down the same tunnels or stepping on the same terrace as some of these relatives.

There are intriguing and courageous transatlantic migratory decisions that changed the destiny of whole families and future generations. Essentially, those on both the Brown and Lambie sides made bold, brave choices to pick up and make a new life for their family in different parts of the world where nothing was certain. They followed their instincts.

As long as there was hope, and as long as they were not afraid to put their nose to the grindstone, anything was possible. Sacrifices were made, but you grow up with the idea that if you believe so passionately about something then you go for it. You never know how it'll turn out, but you still give it your best. You've already won by believing in yourself, your family, and your choice – no matter what it happens to be. Only regret the things you don't do. If you never try, you'll never know.

I grew up with that train of thought, watching my parents make decisions to move to different parts of the world because of various career or entrepreneurial choices. It exposed me to a wonderful view of the world and different cultures and traditions that I might never have experienced if I had just stayed put in one particular region of the US. I'm excited about the idea of imparting that knowledge and tradition to my son.

The focus starts in Troon, Scotland, with a teenage James Brown forging a new path to the United States. The narrative then expands to immediate Troon Brown family brothers and their offspring, and finally to the extended Lambie family down in South Africa. I always knew how talented this side of the family was, but I was only able to envision a 'skeletal framework' of our relatives based on these stories passed down the line.

After the majority of the research had been found digitally while I was in the south of France in Antibes around 2015 and 2016, I also began to gather personal comments and situations about each of these men in my family, penned by writers from back in their time as well as historians from various football clubs, former team-mates, and family. At the same time, I contacted my father, George Brown, on a nearly daily basis, recounting how I had found such-and-such article or photo or made a contact with a club. He would invariably start telling me more about the items that I mentioned to him, and those were the diamonds in the rough that I would make note of and methodically document to essentially polish over and over. Ten pages suddenly became 20, 50, sometimes 80 pages of notes and summaries of the articles I found, sprinkled with great memories from dad and other members of the family. The research odyssey even led me to a point where one cousin informed me that I had another cousin, Andrew Lambie (on the US side of the Lambies), who had lived in Paris for over 30 years; though I had been in France for 20 years, I had never previously known about or met him, so what a joy! We were both retracing the Lambie family tree at the same time and were able to complement and help one another complete certain areas.

It was then time to head out and visit, to absorb the atmosphere where these relatives played, trained, or spent some of the most creative moments of their careers. I traced my grandfather James Brown and his steps through life: passing by the factory in Plainfield, New Jersey, where he first worked as a teenager and where he first laced up his boots for the local soccer team when arriving in the United States in 1927; walking down the only tunnel at Old Trafford that he walked through in the early 1930s as a soccer player at Manchester United; wandering transformed streets and apartment lots in Guildford City and imagining the electricity of the non-league team's dominance and desire to keep winning and move up to the Third Division while war loomed in the late 1930s; and huddling around the only brick in the Tottenham Hotspur dressing room where he suited up.

The hope is that you enjoy this fascinating adventure as much as I have while sifting through newspaper archives and boxes of family photos, contacting club historians and memorabilia collectors, and talking with many members of the family. Along the way, I assembled as many of the pieces of the puzzle as possible. The time spent has allowed me to know more about the Brown and Lambie clans and to reconnect with family members – or, in some cases, to connect for the first time with family members that I didn't know before.

I want to thank all of those who spent countless hours talking about the family and providing their own thoughts about our families and who helped me keep moving forward.

This journey has helped me to grow from a family tree documenter into a public soccer historian as I've combined my long-standing love for soccer and ever-growing love for rugby and family. Along the way, I've become the current vice-president of the Society for American Soccer History. I now view myself as a soccer detective and relish the opportunity to work with other football historical societies throughout the world to help them learn more about players or teams who might have played in the US during specific periods. I want to send special thanks to all family and friends who have listened to me along the way about this research.

Scottish Origins

WITHOUT ANY pregnancy support services closer to home, Isabella Bell Brown and her husband James Brown spent New Year's Eve 1908 at a hospital in Kilmarnock, Scotland. Married three years earlier, the young couple lived on Scotland's south-west coast in the port town of Troon. They had celebrated hours before the calendar turned over from 1908 to 1909 ten miles inland as Isabella gave birth to their new son, James 'Jimmy' Brown. Jimmy entered a rapidly growing family that eventually grew to include three brothers and four sisters: Isabella (Bella), Sarah (Sadie), Jennie, Andrew, John, Martha, and Thomas (Tom).

The elder James Brown was a renowned water polo player, and he would later serve as a balloonist during World War One. At this point of his life, though, he toiled away as a ship labourer and suffered through alcoholism. Regularly away from home for long periods on the sea, James was only sporadically present in the household. It was rumoured that, upon one return, James was threatened and told to stay away because his visits too often ended in Isabella getting pregnant with no means to support another child. Unwelcome back home in Troon, James crossed the Atlantic in 1920 and settled near his brother Robert McCulloch Brown and other Browns who had immigrated to Westfield, New Jersey, to start a new life in the United States.

Growing up in a large working-class family meant that Jimmy and his brothers were expected to contribute to the household income as soon as possible. In addition to the immediate support they offered, James and Isabella both felt that it was extremely important for all the children to look at apprenticeships as a way of helping to secure a means to provide for their future families. With James no longer present in the house, it became even more imperative that every family member earn their keep.

Sent out at the earliest opportunity to learn a trade, Jimmy was 13 years old when he started his apprenticeship in 1922 as a ship's riveter for the Ailsa Shipbuilding Company at Troon Shipyard. During the 1920s, the main customer of the shipyard was the General Steam Navigation Company, which commissioned several coasters from Ailsa. This led to further orders for other coasters, coastal liners, and paddlers.

Jimmy's teenage years thus settled into a familiar rhythm that wove themselves into the fabric of daily family life. Midway through his five-year apprenticeship, Jimmy started to play street soccer in Troon with a group known as the Cookie Rasslers every day after completing his long hours at the shipyard. Playing with anything they could find that would roll along the ground, these first kick-abouts set in motion a lifelong love affair with the sport.

For Jimmy, though, that love affair would take its first full flame across the Atlantic from his native land.

From Street Soccer to the Big Leagues

AT THE completion of his apprenticeship at the Troon Shipyard in 1927, 18-year-old Jimmy made the fateful decision to join his father in the USA. He applied for an immigration visa on 28 October and set sail for New York on the cruise liner SS *Cameronia* on 5 November. Nine days later, Jimmy set foot on US soil for the first time. Initially living with his uncle Robert while he settled into his new American life, Jimmy found work in a factory in Plainfield where he applied the skills learned during his apprenticeship fabricating metal boxes. Despite his own constant attempts to make contact and the additional efforts of his uncle, Jimmy never was able to renew ties with his father after he arrived in the United States. It took a lot of courage to not pack up his pride and head back to Troon where the safety and comfort of his family waited for him. His father did give him something invaluable, though, which you'll learn about later on.

Soon Jimmy also found himself hanging around after work, watching local soccer matches between factory teams. With only a few years of informal street soccer back in Scotland under his belt, Jimmy made his first forays into organised games in New Jersey during the winter of 1928. He first appeared in a match for Plainfield Soccer Club on 26

March 1928 at Mack Field against Hawthorne's of Elizabeth. Plainfield were determined from the start, and the team's new inside-left played a leading role in victory. Breaking through the defence and beating the goalkeeper for his first of three goals that day, Jimmy hit what the *Plainfield Courier-News* called 'a spectacular shot that few players make'. Plainfield went on to a 4-1 victory on the strength of Jimmy's hat-trick.

A week later, Jimmy lined up again with Plainfield for a match against the crew of the steamboat SS *Berengaria*. A common practice at the time, the cruise liner's team played in local leagues while docked in New York. The steamboaters went on the offensive immediately while Plainfield sat back into a 'carpet game' at Mack Field. The drylanders took an early lead but could not hold back the blistering attacks of the *Berengaria* team. Down 4-1 at half-time, Plainfield worked the ball creatively on the attack and netted two goals with the wind at their backs. Jimmy got on the scoresheet, plucking a lucky goal after his team-mate Chapman hit the crossbar on a second-half counter-attack. Plainfield fell short in the 4-3 defeat, but Jimmy showed promise despite his relative lack of formal training.

Jimmy soon heard about the Bayonne Rovers in nearby Bayonne, a strong amateur club playing in the Northern New Jersey League. During a 1994 interview late in his life, Jimmy talked about how he went to watch Bayonne and got to know some of the players. At some point the players asked Jimmy if he wanted to show them what he could do, an offer he couldn't refuse. Jimmy went on to say in the interview that he felt he was quite a good amateur player and better than most of the men on the team, even though they were a good amateur side

Rovers boasted the presence of 16-year-old Henry 'Razzo' Carroll who, although still in high school, was selected to play for the US team at the 1928 Amsterdam Olympics. Playing alongside Carroll, fresh back from a disappointing Olympic tournament in Europe, Jimmy appeared for Rovers for the first time in May in a 3-2 loss against Bayonne Hispano in the first leg of the Northern New Jersey Cup at Marion Oval. In the story on the game in the *Bayonne Courier*, Jimmy was heralded as a 'fiery thatched lad' who 'on more than one occasion … forced the Hispano goal defenders to extend themselves' while playing at outside-left for Rovers.

Jimmy continued to play for Rovers through the summer of 1928. During these young years, he was a hustler with impressive physical advantages in his height and speed that were coupled with a natural instinct for the sport which was quite rare for a teenager. That skill and instinct was soon noticed by the American Soccer League, and on 15 September the *Bayonne Courier* reported that 'Red' Brown was heading 'like a house afire' for Newark of the American League. Less than a year after arriving in the United States, Jimmy Brown embarked on a new career path as a professional soccer player.

Going Pro in the Middle of the Soccer War

IN THE mid-1920s, the American Soccer League (ASL) and the United States Soccer Federation (USFA) battled over jurisdictional issues. Charles Stoneham, the president of the National Exhibition Company and owner of the New York Giants baseball franchise, entered the ASL when he purchased the Indiana Flooring team in 1927. Rebranding Indiana Flooring as the New York Nationals, Stoneham felt that US soccer could be as popular as the European game. He advocated for modern stadiums, well-balanced teams with high-class players, strong affiliations with baseball ownerships, non-conflicting schedules, a new Midwestern league, and a break from the affiliation with the USFA.

With Stoneham leading the way, the ASL fought their obligation to participate in the National Challenge Cup (currently known as the Lamar Hunt US Open Cup), as it disrupted the regular-season matches and created a parallel schedule to manage. At the same time, the ASL had been poaching European players with large contracts, giving the USFA ammunition to sanction the league and place limitations on player signings.

The ASL, unhappy about the sanctions and limitations, withdrew from the 1928/29 National Challenge Cup. Newark exacerbated the situation when, along with powerhouse clubs Bethlehem Steel and New York Giants, they defied the league's boycott of the National Challenge Cup. This was described as the 'Soccer War' in the press. In the first two weeks of September, the ASL suspended the three rebel teams from league competition.

Needing more revenue than participation in the National Challenge Cup could provide, the three suspended ASL clubs joined forces with a handful of other teams – including the former Vienna Hakoah players who founded the famous New York Hakoah club – to form the Eastern Professional Soccer League (ESL), which ran parallel with the established league. Both the ESL and ASL suffered terrible financial losses during their respective 1928/29 campaigns. Over the course of the season, Newark ended up ninth in the ESL and were never higher than fourth. The Skeeters also made it to the quarter-finals of the National Challenge Cup.

Jimmy played an integral role in what successes the Skeeters did enjoy over the course of what proved to be their final season before they folded in the autumn of 1929, when the ASL and ESL merged. With Bayonne Rovers, he had scored one goal in each game played. Upon turning pro with the Newark Skeeters in September 1928, he made 42 appearances and scored 12 goals through a 1928/29 season that included ASL, ESL and National Challenge Cup matches.

Jimmy's first match with Newark was an unfortunate 8-1 loss to the reigning national champions, the New York Nationals, on 2 September. Non-stop pressure resulted in three first-half goals and then five more in the second half. Two Nationals recorded hat-tricks. Luckily, Gasquer of Newark scored to avoid a total blank. After another loss to Bethlehem Steel two days later, Jimmy finally scored his first professional goal for Newark in a 2-2 draw against Boston. Newark struggled at the start of the season with a pair of losses at Rhode Island and Massachusetts and a collapse in the return match at home against the Fall River Marksmen.

During this time, James Brown was away from the team for unknown reasons. When he returned to the field, he quickly found his feet. In one ESL game against the New York Giants on 11 November he scored his first hat-trick, leading Newark to a 4-1 win at the Kearny High School grounds in New Jersey. The first half was a busy one for young James. Twenty minutes into the match, he took the ball up the wing and scored. Then, ten minutes later, his impressive individual efforts led to Newark's second goal. Meanwhile, the Newark defence held strong against the Giants' onslaught. In the second half, James took a cross from the right wing and made it 3-0.

As an interesting aside, three members of the Brown family played on or near the Kearny High School grounds. James Brown was the first with the Newark Skeeters in 1928, and both Jim Brown (1987–91) and David Brown (1979–83) played in this space with the Scotch Plains Fanwood High School varsity soccer team.

Newark gained confidence at home as they continued to battle opponents and either steal points, draw, or lose close matches. In November Jimmy appeared in a one-off New Jersey State Cup match with Plainfield against the First German Soccer Club at Mack Field. Plainfield were locally referred to as the 'Queen City lads', as they were up against a stronger and heavier side. The game 'waxed hot' but the Queen City lads were out to win and give it everything they had. Brown added the second goal with a powerful shot but First German equalised and the game went into extra time. In the dying moments the First German goalkeeper backed over his line when a shot was taken and Plainfield claimed a goal. Disputes ensued between the clubs, with Plainfield winning in the end. They were to meet Trenton the following April in the next round.

On 26 November, Newark drew 1-1 with Hispano in the newly created ESL. James opened up the scoring after taking possession of the ball when his team-mate, Hughes, took a free kick in the first half. Six days later in a match against the IRT Rangers, James was one of three goalscorers as Newark took two crucial points. Featuring in his third match in a fortnight, James played against the Hakoah All Stars. Five minutes before the end of the match he 'whipped in a corking drive' from 15 yards out, beating the goalkeeper to level the score.

By 20 December the Newark Skeeters were fourth in the league behind Bethlehem Steel, the New York Giants and the Hakoah All-Stars. Even in defeat, James proved his worth to the Skeeters. Though Newark lost 5-1 to the Giants on Boxing Day, James raced through from the left wing and 'whipped in' the ball past Jock Brown after only six minutes of play to open the scoring. Halfway through the season, James was 18th in the list of leading ESL scorers with eight goals. As the calendar rolled over to 1929, James continued to score for Newark even as they fell down the standings, but once the Skeeters folded he found himself playing one match for Stoneham's New York Nationals. It was with another New York club, however, that James would make his biggest mark as a professional on American soil.

Joining up with the Giants

AFTER HIS short stint with the New York Nationals, James Brown signed a contract with the New York Giants for the 1929/30 season that paid $50 per game. James featured in an attack that also included Davie (or Davey) Brown (no relation) and Shamus O'Brien, a prolific goalscorer in the league. Over the course of the season James went on to score 16 goals in 38 games, coming close to the ratio of one every other game that marked his amateur days with Bayonne Rovers. As a result, he finished as the 18th-highest scorer in the ASL during the 1929/30 season.

The Giants were owned by Maurice Vandeweghe, who had also owned Hakoah until he was obliged to cease ownership in order to comply with ASL regulations after the end of the Soccer War. On 26 January 1930, the Giants fell 4-2 to Hakoah in a rematch of the previous year's National Challenge Cup Final. Hakoah sat first in the league, with New York following closely in second. The Giants fought hard, even after having a player sent off in both the first and second halves. James and Davie Brown scored before half-time, putting the Giants ahead 2-0. James scored a header from a fine Moorhouse corner. The second half was very different for the Giants, though, as James was ordered off the field after hitting opposing left-half Mahrer.

The following day, James scored again in a 6-4 victory over the Brooklyn Wanderers in front of 2,000 spectators at Starlight Park. This time the Giants pulled off a comeback, falling 4-1 behind in the first half before exploding after the interval. His exploits continued into the spring as he scored regularly for the Giants in both ASL matches and the National Challenge Cup.

Perhaps James's finest performance of the season came on 3 March when he scored a hat-trick in front of 2,500 spectators against the New York Nationals. Over the next five weeks, James scored in both matches against Bethlehem Steel before the club disbanded and reconfigured as the New York Yankees. Though James kept scoring, the Giants tumbled in losses against the Fall River Marksmen and the Hakoah All-Stars to close out their campaign. New York finished the 1930 ASL season in eighth, yet even after a disappointing result as a team, James had proven his skills on the pitch and would soon be representing his new country on the biggest stage of all.

Preparing for the 1930 FIFA World Cup

WITH THE founding of the Fédération Internationale de Football Association (FIFA) on 21 May 1904 in France by Robert Guérin and associates, the idea was to create an organisation to provide medical and social assistance through sports. Football would bring countries together. Jules Rimet (who championed FIFA as president and the need for a 'World' Cup) felt the sport was the single common denominator that could bring together 22 people of all walks of life or social status on the pitch; focusing on a common objective for an hour and a half by working together. Rimet felt that sport could break down racial barriers and promote moral progress, along with providing healthy competition and a lot of fun. The 1905 FIFA Congress approved an attempt at organising the first World Cup but there were no candidate countries willing to host at the time.

During a September 2016 interview, Jules Rimet's grandson Yves Rimet said, 'The goal was to bring youth, blue-collar workers, employees and the upper class. It was a social work of art. The first World Cup would bring all of these classes together around the same values and team spirit, personal accomplishment and achieving anything that you set your mind to.'

Jules Rimet and Henri Delaunay went on to create the first World Cup. Jules would lead the French Football Federation (FFF) as its president and later served as FIFA president for over 33 years.

On 28 May 1928, FIFA's Annual Congress in Amsterdam voted to stage the World Cup every four years. The organiser would cover all costs, including stadium renovations, infrastructure construction, lodging, and transportation expenses for participating delegations and referees. At first, six countries proposed their candidature: Hungary, Spain, Italy, Sweden, Holland and Uruguay. By the 1929 Annual Congress in Barcelona, the choice proved an easy one for FIFA and Uruguay was awarded the first world event. For Uruguay, the tournament offered a chance to celebrate its centennial independence and also acknowledged the country's position as the reigning Olympic champions in 1924 and 1928. It also helped that all the other countries withdrew their bids when they refused to cover expenses, while a wealthy businessman and the Uruguayan government proved willing to fully underwrite the event.

In South America, football was not initially played by the local population, but by Britons who migrated to those countries for work. Large groups of immigrants from England came over to work on the continent's mineral supply, and football was their favourite pastime. The first match played under the Football Association (FA) rules in Central or South America took place in 1867 in Buenos Aires, played by a group of British workers. Uruguay was a small country, with a small population. In the 1920s, Uruguay put in place a well-rounded educational system – in addition to literature, mathematics and physics, physical education was included to serve as complete body-and-mind education.

The United States travelled to the first World Cup in Uruguay with 11 other nations: Argentina, Brazil, Bolivia, Chile, Mexico, Paraguay, Peru, Belgium, France, Romania and Yugoslavia (exclusively made up of Serbian players). There were no qualifying matches. None of the European powerhouses except France and Belgium accepted the invitation, arguing that it was too costly in the aftermath of the worldwide stock market crash in 1929 and that European club teams didn't like having their best players absent for over two months. France's star defender Manuel Anatol and the team's regular coach Gaston Barreau couldn't be persuaded to make the trip, but Jules Rimet convinced the FFF to send the French team. Rimet made the trip to Uruguay from Villefranche-sur-Mer, France, on the SS *Conte Verde* with all the European teams, all the while carrying the first World Cup trophy in his bag – the 18-carat solid gold Jules Rimet Trophy designed and created by French sculptor Abel Lafleur.

Organising the Shot-Putters

BACK IN New York, James Brown senior was naturalised as a United States citizen. That paved the way for James junior to declare his intention of becoming a citizen, which made him eligible to play for the US national team. In the spring of 1930 he was selected to represent the United States at the first World Cup after taking part in several fiercely competitive trial matches. He lived as a boarder at 791 East 169th Street in the Bronx.

James joined the US squad, along with three fellow New York Giants team-mates in George Moorhouse, Philip Slone and Shamus O'Brien (O'Brien was selected for the national team but declined because he was not a US citizen). As the ASL season concluded, James prepared to set sail for South America with Moorhouse and Slone. Not making the trip as part of the Giants contingent was prolific goalscorer Davey Brown, who did not participate in the 1930 World Cup trials because of an injury.

During the trials, James had a knack for taking corners with a deceptive inward curve, often taking everyone, including the goalkeeper, by surprise. In one of the trial matches with the US national team against the Brooklyn Wanderers, James delivered one such corner that Billy Gonsalves hammered home. A few minutes later, James scored himself from a corner by Jim Gallagher.

Since everyone on the US side were new to each other, more or less, it took some time to get used to each other's styles and expectations. Billy Gonsalves and Bert Patenaude were true leaders from the get-go. Archie Stark couldn't make the trip because of a new garage repair shop business venture he was setting up with his family. Alec Wood at full-back was 'as safe as the US Treasury'. Phil Slone never knew when he was beat and if you told him that there were still 30 minutes to play, he would say, 'I thought so.' Jimmy Douglas was safe in goal and always managed to feed the ball out to give the forwards something to run on to. James Brown was long, lanky, speedy and strong – he scored two goals. Frank Vaughn, a US national team member, wrote periodic columns for the *St Louis Post-Dispatch*, about the team's preparations, experience in Montevideo and overall impressions between June and September 1930. He said at the end of the match, 'Gee, this overgrown youngster sure can travel.'

On 13 June 1930, James packed his bags, taking special care of the new suit bought for him by the US Soccer Federation for the South American tour. Along with his team-mates – 15 professionals and one amateur of Scottish and English origin – James embarked on the Munson line Pan American cruise liner, the SS *Munargo*, for a historic journey from the local pier on 15th Street in Hoboken, New Jersey, at 6.30am.[1] Soon the team was nicknamed the 'Muscle Men' or 'Shot-putters' by the international press because of their great physical condition. Interestingly, James was not naturalised by the US East District Court

—

1 I ended up, unknowingly, living 100 yards from that very same pier in Hoboken during two years in 1997. Many evenings were spent watching the sunset on the balcony, overlooking the pier, and gazing towards the New York skyline.

in Brooklyn until 15 June – two days after the team set sail for South America. Luckily there were no snags in the application process.

On 23 June, Frank Vaughn wrote about the journey down to South America. They travelled with the Mexican national team on the SS *Western World*, as the one-day delay forced them to change boats when they picked up the Mexicans on the way through the Caribbean. The ocean got rough at some points and 'strangely enough Jimmy Douglas and Arnie Oliver lost their appetites'. The trainer, Jack Coll, was content with a light workout during the voyage. Bob Millar, the manager, although being white-haired, claimed that he could 'outwork any man' in the squad. Bill Cumming, the commander-in-chief of the squad, bought a training outfit – but the whole group wondered why, because he hadn't moved from his deckchair since the voyage began. Captain Tom Florie proved the comedian and Mike Bookie was the 'foil' or source of his wisecracks, but Bookie always took it with a smile. The team were confident, in great shape, and looking forward to proving themselves in South America. They were a small, young and light bunch, averaging no more than 150lb (10st 10lb) per player. Their trainer said that they were very fast but didn't like much 'roughing'.

The US and Mexican delegations arrived in Buenos Aires on 27 June. The US team were hosted as the guests of Botafogo and Santos the following day, then engaged in swimming and baseball practice on the sands of the Santos Harbour beach. They then sailed just before midnight for Montevideo. The team sailed into Montevideo at 1.30pm on 1 July. The day was cold and rainy, but the dreary weather didn't stop crowds and reporters from greeting the Americans at dockside. Marcel Pinel of France recalled that the Americans were huge men with enormous thighs who ran bare-chested around the training track.

The Americans were placed in Group D, along with Paraguay and Belgium. They resumed training on 3 July after having only limited opportunity to exercise on the *Munargo*. A sentiment echoed through the press circles that the US had the best-conditioned team in the competition. On the following morning, the players celebrated Independence Day on foreign soil by leading a parade around the streets of Pocitos, proudly brandishing the Stars and Stripes. Upon their return to the hotel they found Old Glory placed alongside the Uruguayan flag. That afternoon they were guests of Nacional for a match against Missionary, which they won 2-1. That match gave the US the first impression of the South American style.

They attended another local match on the following Sunday, when Peñarol played against River Plate, an Argentine side. There were around 20,000 spectators in attendance. The US had stopped by to visit the new Estadio Centenario, still under construction for the World Cup, and when they got to the game it was already in progress. The match was held up when the US arrived, and the Yanks gave their 'Three Rousing Cheers' to the crowd. The response was 'thunderous and re-echoed for miles!' according to reports. The US sat with the French and Mexican teams at the match. Jules Rimet and vice-president and US representative M. Fischer were in attendance as well.

On 11 July the team were invited to a luncheon and to play golf at the Chimont Golf Club by Swift and Company, an American-owned packing plant located in Uruguay. The official opening ceremony for the tournament took place on 13 July at the newly built Estadio Centenario with all the teams represented, marching out and lining up with their national flag. The US team marched out, singing the 'Stein Song' and carrying the flag. James Brown was the tallest in the group, situated in the back and to the right of the flag.[2]

—

2 Videos of the 1930 World Cup opening ceremony show the US delegation and a clear shot of James Brown, the tallest member of the group, at the back and to the right of the flag. There are no other films of James from the World Cup or any other match in his career.

The Run to the Semi-Finals

FOR THE first game of the World Cup group stages, conditions were dreary and cold. The playing field was a bed of mud with clumps everywhere, and the conditions weren't helped by playing with a heavy leather ball that rapidly became a cannonball with every kick. Belgium were without their best player, Raymond Braine, who scored 141 goals in 142 games in eight years for Beerschot. Braine was banned by the Belgian federation from the tournament after opening a cafe in order to supplement his income – an act that broke Belgian amateurism rules. While the US team were preparing in the dressing room, President Herbert Hoover sent a telegram wishing the squad the best of luck.

They were in good spirits in front of a crowd of 10,000, but the first 20 minutes saw little happening. Midfielders were misdirecting passes and forwards were way off their mark. Finally, James let a lightning shot rip from the right wing. As it crashed against the crossbar, Bart McGhee put it away. Once the first goal was scored, the Americans settled into their game and Tom Florie scored the second before half-time. The match ended in a 3-0 victory for the Americans.

In his official report on the tournament, manager W.R. Cummings wrote that James Brown made 'a beautiful run' on the right wing to set up the third and last goal by Bert Patenaude. When the Belgian goalkeeper left his line to challenge, Brown delivered an 'unselfish lob over the goalkeeper's head' to Patenaude, who headed the ball into an empty net. Cummings described it as 'one of the most brilliant plays in the entire tournament'. In a 1994 ABC Sports interview, James said, 'I was 21, confident, and could run like a deer.' Jimmy Douglas, the US goalkeeper, recorded the first clean sheet of the tournament. James collected the first assist and Bart McGhee the first goal for the US in the World Cup. With that convincing win, they gained momentum and the confidence needed for the next match against Paraguay.

The Paraguayans were considered the 'dark horses' of the tournament after eliminating Argentina and Uruguay from the previous year's South American Championship. Over 20,000 attended the match at Central Park, enjoying crisp but clear weather that proved ideal for the flashy combinations the US put together. The Americans entered the stadium singing the 'Stein Song' and were on the front foot from the opening minute. Paraguay's midfield and attackers could never get anything going and had to watch as Bert Patenaude broke through and 'crashed three markers against the rigging'.

After the group matches, the US were viewed as favourites based on the thrashings they gave Belgium and Paraguay – banging in six goals, recording the first hat-trick by Patenaude against Paraguay,[3] and conceding no goals at

—

3 The first World Cup hat-trick was previously attributed by FIFA to Argentina's Guillermo Stábile, who scored three goals during a match against Mexico two days later in the 1930 World Cup. FIFA finally recognised Bert Patenaude for the first hat-trick in World Cup history in 2006. During the Paraguay game, local newspapers attributed the goals to numerous US team members because of their difficulty in recognising them. The attribution by FIFA came after Colin Jose, a North American soccer historian and collector of World Cup annuals, presented FIFA in 1995 with research including the official manager's report, local newspaper diagrams detailing the path of each goal, and National Soccer Hall of Fame interviews and discussions between Colin and both Arnie Oliver and James Brown supporting the claim.

the other end. They advanced on to the semi-finals against a strong Argentinian side. Brazilian midfielder Hermógenes Fonseca, who attended the US–Paraguay match, told a journalist from the newspaper *Critica* that he thought the American style of play was 'admirable', and that the team were 'clear, fair, intelligent'. Fonseca said the players were fighters, 'robust, fiery, passionate' with 'a discipline almost unbreakable'. 'In the heat of battle,' Fonseca noted that the Americans 'act calmly' and shoot 'very well, with violence and direction'. He also singled out James Brown for his 'terrifying shot, very powerful, a kind of cannon shot'.

The lottery for the semi-finals was conducted on 23 July in the presence of US captain James Gentle, with his team facing Argentina and Uruguay matched against Yugoslavia. On the same day, Argentine newspaper *La Nación* described the Americans as a 'powerful and vigorous team' that was 'strong in all their lines and overwhelming in their attack. No one stays with the ball more than the time required.' The newspaper also praised the American ball movement, arguing that the US passed 'if not with beauty, at least in conjunction with harmony and precision'. On 20 July the team had paid their respects to the memory of General Artigas of Uruguay, placing an everlasting wreath and floral arrangement at the foot of the statue in Independence Square.

The *St Louis Post-Dispatch* newspaper carried a column from Frank Vaughn, offering his impressions of the trial matches and the World Cup fixtures. One column published on 20 July paid particular attention to the treatment of goalkeepers. In South America players were not allowed to charge the goalkeeper, let alone knock him into the goal along with the ball, as was the custom throughout the world at the time. Vaughn felt that the US team would be greatly tempted to charge the goalkeeper, but that he expected many 'razzberries' from the South Americans (the term 'razzberries' was a 1920s reference to the Bronx Cheer: the sound of raspberries the crowd makes to show their disapproval).

After a light training session on 22 July, the team were guests of the Archbishop of Montevideo. Three days later, non-playing members of the US delegation paid a visit to the house of Uruguay's president Juan Campisteguy at Los Predas. They were served barbecued lamb and pork sausages with all the traditional trimmings, wonderful French pastry, and national red and white wines as well as champagne. Then it was back to Montevideo for a concert by the National Band in the lobby of the Carrosco Hotel. During all of these celebrations, the US players remained back at the hotel, 'never wavering from the straight and narrow'.

There was no doubt about the passion for football in South America. Before the semi-final match against Argentina, when the US team walked through the streets, men, women, and even children would yell at them. In terms of the Americans' physical condition, trainer Bob Millar felt that if they could run the incredible length and width of the South American fields, then the wind would take them the rest of the way. Besides, they all knew how to kick a ball, so it was run, run, run. Vaughn lost 22lb in weight during the tour.

Tensions were high, as morning newspapers spoke of how the police were going to frisk everyone – even the players – for knives and guns. The team travelled into the stadium under military horseback escort and then they sang their traditional 'Stein Song'. They were up against a powerful, well-trained Argentinian team that played a ruthless and unforgiving style. In front of more than 112,000 spectators, the US struggled with long passes that were falling short and dropping into their own half. The pitch was at least eight yards over the maximum length allowed, and it showed in the first half. The Americans played in a 'W' formation and had been playing old English-style football, with long lateral passes from wing to wing, but the length of the pitch caused problems for their attacks.

In the first four minutes of the match, US goalkeeper Jimmy Douglas badly twisted his knee, but he 'stuck to his guns' and stopped attack after attack. After the first 20 minutes Ralph Tracey had his right leg fractured[4] and since substitutes weren't allowed at the time in international competitions (though they were allowed in league matches in the United States), the Americans essentially played with two men down for the final 70 minutes. They had only let in one goal by the end of the first half.

Andy Auld had his lip split open – later reports talked of him having three or four teeth knocked out – after the second Argentine goal. As fate would have it, team trainer Jack Coll was coming over to take care of Andy when he was bumped by the opposing side and the smelling salts in his hands flew into Andy's eyes and temporarily blinded the 'little star'. That explains the photo of Andy with a towel in his mouth during the game.

In 1994, James said during an ABC Sports interview that the Argentinians were often picking up mud and throwing it in the US squad's faces. Every thinkable combination of position changes and tactics did no good as the Argentinians continued to slash from left to right and racked up a 6-0 lead. In the 89th minute, the temporarily blinded Auld executed a 'hair-raising' individual performance to find Brown with

—

4 There are questions about whether Tracey broke his leg because he couldn't have continued playing for as long as he did, and there was no cast on his leg in photos taken later during the tour. In a *St Louis Post-Dispatch* interview on 7 September 1930, Frank Vaughn spoke of his team-mate 'having a badly wrenched knee' when he tried to clear a ball and an Argentine player leapt at him, hitting him on his left knee.

a pass. James neatly put it away and the Americans got on the scoresheet in a 6-1 defeat. If there had been fair play and better refereeing – along with substitutions, which continued to be banned by FIFA until the 1970 World Cup – the score and outcome could have been drastically different.

Returning Home from Uruguay

FOR ALL their efforts, the US ended up winning the bronze medal, ahead of Yugoslavia, based on goal difference. There has been talk that the Yugoslavian team refused to play the third-place match and were therefore given fourth position, though unofficial reports later mentioned that the captains of both the US and Yugoslavian teams were given third-place medals. Players received their medals at home, by mail, as the US didn't have time to get together when arriving home. Bert Patenaude was the third-highest scorer of the tournament with four goals. The Americans ranked fourth in terms of the highest total game attendances, with over 142,000 spectators at their three matches, where they demonstrated their strength, speed, hard work, intelligence and creativity on the pitch.

After the World Cup, the US squad remained in South America until the third week in August. During their extended time away from home the team squared off in seven exhibition games against professional clubs in Brazil and Uruguay. James scored in the last night game against Botafogo in Rio de Janeiro on 19 August – exactly five years to the day before his second son, George, joined the family.

Then the US made their way home on the SS *Southern Cross* cruise liner with the Hakoah All-Stars team, who had been touring South America since mid-June, and the Americans were satisfied with their successful South American tour. Hakoah's trip was less profitable than anticipated, and their players were forced to stay in the cheapest accommodation. James often took food down to the Hakoah players on the return voyage. During his 1994 interview with ABC Sports, James said, 'These [US team] players were a splendid mixture of America.' In more lucid days, he was able to recite all the players, US or Hakoah, from goalkeeper to the forward line.

The Americans docked in New York, disembarking from the *Southern Cross* on 2 September. A 7 September *St Louis Post-Dispatch* interview with Frank Vaughn talked about how South American teams were 'poor losers' and how referees interpreted rules differently depending on where they came from. For example, you couldn't 'shoulder' other players, but opponents could leap at you, and that's how Ralph Tracey received the serious, perhaps career-ending, knee injury. Tracey, Andy Auld and Jimmy Douglas were all hospitalised in New York upon their return. During throw-ins players had to stand flat-footed and face towards the opponents' goal. The goalkeeper could bounce the ball up until the edge of the penalty box and couldn't be challenged. Referees relied on linesmen to make the calls for fouls and penalties most of the time.

Officiating peculiarities manifested again at a local exhibition match in Brazil on the return home from the World Cup. Referees called clear goals as offsides. They lost their composure and got into arguments on the field with players. One goal was awarded by the referee, and he pointed to the halfway line – but when the opposing team surrounded him and verbally attacked him, he simply reversed his decision and called it a goal kick. A linesman ran on to the field and kissed a local team's player when he scored a goal.

At the USFA's 18th annual meeting at the Palmer House in Chicago, Illinois in late June 1931, treasurer W.R. Cummings articulated to the president and committee how disappointed he was with the officiating during the exhibition matches after the World Cup. Cummings stated that he wouldn't do it again for $50,000 but was nonetheless honoured to have been selected to lead the South American tour.

The Post-World Cup Windfall

EVEN BEFORE returning to the US after the World Cup, there were reports of negotiations between James and several professional clubs in the United Kingdom: Glasgow Rangers, Everton and Newcastle United. The autumn of 1930 brought James back to his club, New York Giants, only to find that the name had been changed to New York Soccer Club or New York SC, where he scored six goals in 25 appearances. New York had a nice passing game and were strong in defence. On 8 September New York Soccer Club battled New Bedford in Massachusetts in the opening game of the season and recorded a decisive 6-1 victory. James scored during the collective effort. A week later, New York played Hakoah, who had just come back from a South American tour and lost 1-0 in a tight match. From the opening whistle the pace was terrific, as the ball went with lightning-like speed up and down the field. Moorhouse and Glover did their best to prevent more goals from finding their way into the back of the New York net.

The 29 September match against the Brooklyn Wanderers found Davie Brown in great shape, netting a hat-trick. James hammered the nail in the coffin as New York SC won handily, 4-0. James was busy, assisting one goal with a lovely cross from the right wing and then heading in from a corner from Andy Horne in the second half. Four days after that match it was reported that James was to have his tonsils taken out, but that he was going to wait until a situation concerning another player cleared up – a sign that even soccer had its rumour columns during this period.

On 27 October, Fall River squared off against New York. Four former 1930 World Cup team-mates found themselves on opposite sides of the field: Fall River's Bert Patenaude and Billy Gonsalves faced George Moorhouse and James Brown in the ASL match at Starlight Park before 2,000 spectators. It was a well-fought match that should have resulted in more goals, but Fall River came out ahead and won 2-1.

In late November, the *New Jersey Courier News* reported on the composition of the New York Soccer Club in their match versus the Newark Americans. For New York, Jock Brown – the country's best (singing) goalkeeper – was guarding the sticks. Davey Brown, a popular favourite in the New York/New Jersey league, slotted in on the forward line alongside 'big' James Brown, who did so well during the All-American South American tour a few months earlier. Moorhouse, the outstanding full-back who had a sensational tour with the US team in Montevideo, proved a stalwart in defence.

Brown's play 'was sensational in both halves' as New York SC beat Fall River 1-0. In the match played up in Fall River, Massachusetts, Andy Horne put in a strong effort with James assisting the forward line over the course of the 90 minutes. Just a few days before 1930 concluded, New York SC defeated New Bedford 4-3 in front of 1,500 spectators after a snowstorm left the field in dire condition. James and Davey, referred to in the press as the 'Brown Brothers' despite there being no relation, netted one goal each. James scored the third of New York's four goals after only 17 minutes of play.

In January 1931, in what was billed as 'the biggest soccer trade of the season', James was sent to the Brooklyn Wanderers where he made 31 appearances and scored ten goals. He was described as a youngster of great promise and said to possess everything that a first-class forward ought to have. On the flipside, among the compliments also appeared the specific frustration that James had not been playing 'at his best consistently'. An interesting side note is that he was recruited to play for Brooklyn at the same time as his old Bayonne Rovers team-mate and former 1928 Olympian, Henry 'Razzo' Carroll. Razzo only played eight games with the Wanderers, but seven of his appearances took place alongside James. Isaac Gellis of the *New York Evening Post* reported on 27 January, 'Although not being a finished product yet, James has shown remarkable skill and promise.' In February 1931, Nat Agar – the manager of the Brooklyn Wanderers – said that James was 'unusual' as he could play either wing position on the forward line. He was young, tall, and a great player 'when in the mood'.

James wasn't eligible to play right away with Brooklyn, so he participated in a charity game on 13 February for the benefit of New York mayor James John Walker's Unemployment Fund. The match raised $800. The teams were made up of Americans and foreigners, called the Europeans. The Americans were 3-0 ahead at half-time. During the interval, the players on both sides walked into their respective dressing rooms completely covered in mud. Every man played their heart out and by the end of the match it was virtually impossible to distinguish one team from another. Jock Brown, the winning side's goalkeeper, was mistaken for the Europeans' Pepi Schneider, and was consoled as he passed the spectators.

The American team was an almost carbon copy of the national team from the 1930 World Cup, but interestingly enough, James was included with the native-born Americans and not the Europeans. The Americans seemed to enjoy playing again on the same side, as opposed to slugging it out week in, week out, with eight of the World Cup side – Alexander Wood, George Moorhouse, James Gallagher, Andy Auld, James Brown, Billy Gonsalves, Bert Patenaude and Bart McGhee – making the squad. Shamus O'Brien was in the line-up as well, along with Razzo Carroll. Goals were scored by O'Brien, Gonsalves, Patenaude, Brown and Carroll. The Europeans scored twice from corners.

At this confusing point during the season, the Fall River Marksmen were financially suffering, and owner Sam Mark decided to close up shop and move down to New York. In the process, Mark merged the Fall River Marksmen with the New York Soccer Club to form the New York Yankees soccer team. In a match against the newly formed Yankees at Starlight Park on 15 March, Brooklyn were sent packing in a 5-0 drubbing. Billy Gonsalves led the charge with two goals, Scotty Nilsen also scored a brace, and Tec White completed the scoring. Brooklyn made a brave attempt to open the home season with a victory over Pawtucket on 16 March, reinforced by their latest acquisitions, James Brown, Carroll, and Boland. Despite the efforts, with four corners taken in the second half, they lost 1-0.

James never shied away from a challenge, though. Brooklyn came up against the powerful and dominant Fall River on 12 April. The Wanderers took advantage of four corners in the first half, James scoring in the first ten minutes from a pass by Devlin. He drove the ball unerringly past the Fall River goalkeeper. Brown completed his brace and secured the winning goal with a 'nice header' from another corner as Brooklyn won 2-1.

In a match against Hakoah on 13 April, goalkeeper Louis Fisher was doing his level best to stop everything that came his way, including two sensational saves on shots from Brown. Then, in the last period, James caught the exceptional goalkeeper 'unaware'. During the match James collided with a Hakoah full-back, which caused a deep cut under his opponent's eye and left James badly shaken up as well. By that point in the match, most of the Hakoah 11 were 'hobbling around'. At the end of the season, on 1 June, Brooklyn finished in second place behind the New York Giants, 'nosing out' the Yankees in the process. They defeated the Newark Americans 4-0 in their final match, with James scoring.

Next up for Brooklyn was an exhibition match against the touring Scottish champions Glasgow Celtic on 8 June. Over 10,000 spectators saw Celtic rip into the New York side, winning in a convincing 5-0 romp. Glasgow didn't leave empty handed – as was the custom, when touring teams fancied a player, they would try and sign him and take him back with them. That was the case with James M'Guire, the Brooklyn centre-half. He gave such a fine display in recent matches that Glasgow had to get him. He was originally from Edinburgh, Scotland, so it wasn't completely new territory for him.

At the end of spring 1931, the Brooklyn Wanderers folded. During the summer months, James kept busy playing with Port Chester and he was part of the team when they won a five-a-side tournament on 4 July. He won another five-a-side tournament with Nassau later in the summer. James was shown in the line-up with the Newark Americans during their 5-2 defeat to Hakoah on 27 November. Newark finished the 1931/32 season in seventh place.

After the success on the professional soccer field, James advanced on the personal playing field with Mary Ann Cormack. Born on 11 February 1911 in Helmsdale, Scotland, Mary grew up in Bower before moving to the United States aged 16. Mary arrived on 2 July 1927 on the SS *Caledonia* with her parents, Alexander and Isabella Cormack. Mary and James met after the World Cup in late 1930, possibly at a soccer match. One possible connection was Isobel Hamilton, the wife of Mary's brother George Cormack, who came from around Troon. According to the 1930 US Census, Mary worked in Manhattan as a scullery maid at a New York estate on Fifth Avenue that was owned by Sidney Mitchell, an investment banker, and his wife, Alicia Bella. Mary was responsible for cleaning out the fireplace at 5am, all of the kitchen tools, and other tasks. She was still single at the time. The Cormacks had settled in Smithtown, Long Island. James and Mary were married sometime after the World Cup, perhaps in 1931.

The better part of 1932 saw James playing with the Newark Americans, renamed in late March or early April as Newark City. On 10 January, James scored in the first half of the Newark Americans' 4-1 defeat of the Newark Portuguese during the annual USFA National Challenge Cup at Clark's Field. The 8 February semi-final drew the Newark Americans against the reigning national champions, New York Giants, who hoped to march towards a second title. Over 3,000 spectators witnessed a forceful, muddy match in the Eastern finals, as the Giants netted six goals. Just as he had a year and a half earlier at the World Cup, James managed to slip in the lone goal for Newark. James's former 1930 World Cup team-mates played a key role in Newark's defeat, with Bert Patenaude completing a hat-trick and Jimmy Gallagher adding another goal in the semi-final.

On 4 April, James scored as Newark City drew 2-2 with the New York Americans. More than 2,000 spectators at Starlight Park in New York witnessed a thrilling match that saw Newark take a two-goal lead and hold it until the final ten minutes. Two weeks later, James appeared again for Newark City for a 5-1 exhibition rout of his old buddies at Port Chester, scoring on the baseball grounds. His last recorded appearance for Newark took place on 25 April, a 4-0 exhibition defeat against the New York Americans.

Returning to the Source

BECAUSE OF his impressive performances at the 1930 World Cup and his continued progression in the US professional league, James caught the eye of some English league teams. Scott Duncan, the newly appointed secretary-manager of Manchester United, was especially interested in James. Duncan was close friends with the secretary of the New York Soccer Association, Mr Hollywood, who recommended James to the club. In 1932 the American Soccer League was on its way down and out, so James took advantage of the interest from across the Atlantic and returned to the United Kingdom. Before leaving, he took part in the Round Hill Games and won the 100-yard dash in July.

Duncan had hopes of intercepting the *Caledonia* cruise liner that was carrying Brown. As Duncan made his way up the country to meet James, he kept on bumping into Donald Turner, the trainer of Partick Thistle – the team of James's uncle, Alex Lambie, Thistle's former captain. Turner knew then that it was no coincidence; they were after the same player.

Sitting at a restaurant one morning having tea in Greenock, Duncan saw a glimpse of the *Caledonia* coming around the corner. He knew he wouldn't be alone but didn't expect there to be so much interest from other teams. Duncan had a stroke of genius, though, as he paid a tugboat captain to take him out to the *Caledonia* to meet (and sign) Brown before arriving at the port. He raced up the gangway, thinking he had beaten everyone to the punch. Once he arrived on the *Caledonia*, though, Duncan saw Donald Turner ushering Brown into a purser's room and closing the door. Duncan rushed in and, within a few minutes, whisked James away to the chief steward's room to sign a contract with the Red Devils. The transfer fee to the Brooklyn Wanderers was estimated to be around £1,700.

It is not known for certain, but there were rumours that a middleman in the US received a payment for Brown's transfer to Manchester United. James learned about it later on and wasn't happy that he didn't get a signing bonus. Nevertheless, Duncan came down the gangway with a signed contract in hand, Brown at his side, and a smirk from ear to ear as he passed William McCartney, the other strongly interested manager, who had sent a wire asking for a meeting with James when he arrived. McCartney looked on helplessly, alongside the other managers at the port, as Duncan and James passed.

Manchester United saw declining and worrisome years in the early 1930s. The 1930/31 season saw United relegated from the First Division after finishing in 22nd place. The relegation, coupled with the severe effects of the Great Depression, hurt the team at the gates and impacted the financial stability of the club. The 1931/32 season in the Second Division saw a change of direction as manager Herbert Bamlett left and secretary Walter Crickmer took over team affairs. By December 1931, players were no longer getting paid and bankruptcy was right around the corner. The club's saving grace came in the form of James Gibson, a manufacturer of army uniforms. He invested £30,000 to take care of the player, salaries and all outstanding debts. He appointed a new manager, Scott Duncan, who had a large purse with which to engineer United's return to the First Division. They ended the 1931/32 season in 12th place.

Reporters wrote that James was a 'brilliant' outside-right and considered to be a second Alex Jackson, a highly talented Scottish-born footballer known for his dribbling and free kicks. Jackson had featured for Bethlehem Steel in Pennsylvania before returning to Britain, where he notably scored 70 goals in 179 appearances for Huddersfield Town. In his first match with Manchester United, on 17 September 1932, James marked his debut against Grimsby with a hell of a bang. James scored an impressive goal directly from a corner, with the wind blowing away from the goal and swerving in at almost a right angle. A columnist from the *Manchester Evening Chronicle* wrote that James received a standing ovation from over 12,000 spectators at the start of the match. He was able to shoot with either foot surprisingly hard, one reporter wrote, and was an athlete from head to toe. James gave away a free kick when he first touched the ball, but immediately came back and performed well in a 1-1 draw against Grimsby.

Forwards were there to score and help keep the team at the top of the league, to win championships, or secure promotions. When they did, they often received small weekly bonuses. But this system caused tension between team-mates because some 'star' players would get more than others. This could slowly poison the spirit of any team, especially if they slipped further and further down towards relegation. In those days, game pay consisted of around £5 to £7 and an additional £2 bonus for a win.[5] It's been said that for a Wembley international in the early 1930s, the FA paid the

—

5 This is equivalent to $480 or €400 per win in 2022.

band that provided the pre-match entertainment more than they paid the England team.

Being dropped into the reserves meant a significant loss of wages. If you were in the 'stiffs', your pay might drop further to £4 per week. Once out of the first and second teams, the extra bonuses for wins and draws disappeared as well. Summer, non-playing months were usually paid at £4, or some teams would not re-sign a player at the end of the season and then re-hire him at the start of the autumn season to avoid summer payments. Upon re-signing players for the new season, the conditions of the contract weren't always the same as they were at the end of the previous campaign. In the early 1930s many professional players were forced to seek unemployment, not because of lack of spots in the squad but because clubs were keeping more and more players on the retain-and-transfer list. This allowed them to avoid paying players at all. So, for as long as the players stayed on the list, they were forced to play (work) for free.

There were four Scots at Old Trafford at the start of the 1932 season: Frame, Brown, Chalmers and Stewart. There was electricity in the air and a feeling that attractive and interesting football was just around the corner. The camaraderie within the first team was a good sign of the efforts they would make on the field as a unit. Compliments came flooding in, though so did the occasional reprimand. While on the bus to an away game, Mary Brown was given 'a good talking to' by the wife of the centre-forward who James had replaced in the starting line-up and had thus robbed them of proper wages. Even though Manchester United struggled during the early 1930s, you wouldn't have sensed it when you read through the official match programmes. Training in those days consisted of more 'endless' running around the field and a lot of stretching, muscle work and gymnastics, so that the players were able to avoid injury. Touching a ball during practice 'was a treat'. Trainers had to find ways of acting as physiotherapists as well. It was described that a normal remedy for cuts was iodine; for sprains the go-to approach was whiskey.

In the autumn of his first season with Manchester United, James was praised equally for his assists as he was for the creative goals he scored. Against Oldham Athletic on 24 September, Brown was badly neglected as the new outside-right, though he was 'always dangerous' when he secured the ball. The overall game was uninteresting with missed chances, such as a slow inside pass from Brown to Gallimore that ended up over the bar. Charlie Roberts, a journalist in the Manchester area, wrote that he was 'a little disappointed' by Brown. After hearing so much praise for Brown – with some saying he was as good as Meredith – Roberts felt that he needed to speed up considerably and that, being very deliberate in all he did on the pitch, Brown sometimes hesitated in English football. Even so, Roberts acknowledged that Brown possessed good, cool judgement and two-footed skill, making him a valuable addition to the United staff. He was versatile enough and had the height and weight – at just over six feet tall and 12st (168lb) – to play elsewhere in the attack if needed, though he played chiefly at outside-right and preferred that position.

On the leisure side, James was passionate about golf. As a naturally gifted long hitter, he had been playing since he was five years old across the way at the Troon Golf Club. He was told that, since arriving at Manchester United, he had the longest drive at the Chorlton course in Manchester. He developed long hitting while playing golf in the US, where he found he had a natural swing. In 1932 his handicap was about eight, and his longest drive was 360 yards. He carried ten clubs, and his favourite – apart from the driver – was the three iron.

Comparing the English style to the US, James said, 'English football is clever and more methodical than American football, but it's not faster and it's not so vigorous.' He was not at all perturbed by the pace of his first game, as he had done a lot of sprinting and won prizes in Scottish sporting events in the US.

By October, James was gaining success and praise as an outside-right for United. Against Burnley on 8 October, he was the best forward on his side and was able to control the ball quickly and with steady nerves. James equalised Burnley's goal with a strong header from Spence's corner. Willighan, the Burnley defender, was badly hurt after tackling Brown rather indiscreetly, and came on to the pitch after the interval limping. United came more into focus and Burnley began to waver badly. James assisted a goal and missed out on scoring a second when he tried to turn a corner into the net but was blocked on the line by a Burnley defender. In their next game, against Preston North End, he didn't get the ball often, but when he did, 'something interesting always happened'.

A week later, Bradford took advantage of a strong breeze to go ahead 1-0 in the first half. After working the ball well up the field, United gained their first corner, which Brown overhit. Brown 'placed the ball admirably' from their next corner, but further efforts were off target. The crowd showed their discontent, and Brown's own disappointment was visible as well.

Against Millwall on 22 October, United romped to a lopsided 7-1 victory as James showed happier traces of 'the Brown of early on' from his first Old Trafford match as he scored one goal and added two partial – and unintentional –

assists. His goal came with a hard shot that ended up in the back of the net in the 38th minute, and just after the hour his corner resulted in a goal by Gallimore. The last contribution from James came five minutes after Gallimore's goal, when he dribbled nearly half the length of the field and rocketed a shot on target; the ensuing clearance fell to his fellow attacker Reid to tuck away.

At the beginning of November against Notts County, James assisted from a corner. Soon after, he missed a great chance in the 22nd minute from two yards out. This was not his best day, as he found himself 'losing faith' in his left foot and passing to others who were less well-positioned for a shot. The *Manchester Evening News* quoted James as saying that it was about the worst game he had ever had and that 'his two feet were like lead'. The writer finished it off by saying that it certainly can rain in England!

The rest of November went better for James. In the match against Bury on 12 November, he kicked like a rugby three-quarter and eventually headed in a spectacular goal. He posted a rather 'grand goal' in front of a crowd of over 30,000 against Fulham on 19 November from a pass by Ridding. Four minutes later, James repaid the favour with a magnificent run through the Fulham defence and a lay-off for Ridding to complete the 'child's task' of finishing.

James rarely received a good pass in the final match of November against Chesterfield as the midfield struggled through a sluggish afternoon. Along with Stewart, James kept putting on bursts of speed through the Chesterfield defence, coming in wave after wave as they tried to open the scoring. James was finally rewarded for his efforts on the hour when he beat everybody with a glorious run, cut in towards the goal, and squarely passed on to Ridding at the far post.

A mid-December game against West Ham United showed moments where James lacked anticipation in the penalty box, though he made up for it with a centre to assist the only goal. He narrowly missed from a bad angle and was credited as one of most effective United forwards on the day, forcing the West Ham goalkeeper to save brilliantly from a last-minute corner. The following weekend against Lincoln City, James laid the preliminary 'spadework' for two goals as his long, raking strides deceived defenders of his true pace.[6] Brown sent in a corner that Reid took advantage of to score his first of three goals on the day. Reid's second came as Brown cleverly beat Lincoln's Smith and crossed beautifully to Reid, who then headed it in. On Christmas Eve against Swansea Town, Brown scored the only goal as Manchester United lost 2-1 after travelling more than 225 miles by train and taxi. United settled in and fought hard against Swansea, with Stewart centring to Brown, who had wandered into the middle for an easy finish.

A 31 December *Manchester Evening Chronicle* article – published on Brown's 24th birthday – argued that against Plymouth, James wasn't up to his early form. The columnist mentioned that he 'always admired' James's enthusiasm, but that he 'has been recently slow and hesitant in getting his centres'. The article went on to admit that he certainly did well scoring against Swansea.

The shift from 1932 to 1933 came with more challenges. James displayed a 'strange ineptitude' on a rather cold and rainy day on 27 January against Tottenham Hotspur. He didn't warm up for the game and was utterly distrustful of

6 This 'raking strides' comment was often made by his son George when he talked about his father's simple yet deceptive style. Not step-overs, but feints to the left and right, combined with bursts of speed, throwing defenders into the crowds. He did force the offside ruling a bit too often, though, getting caught and having goals disallowed.

the slippery surface. A month later, James was playing for the United reserve team as they were hammered 4-1 by Burnley's reserves. The Burnley men proved lighter and nippier than United's charges. James's fellow forward, Black, almost got United on the scoreboard. James crossed and Black headed towards goal, but it was not to be as the effort was easily saved.

Fortunes turned again as winter shifted to spring, with most of the April match reports noting that Brown had greatly improved after his cold spell. In the return match against Chesterfield on 8 April, Brown used the ball well, cut in with great determination, and had a few shots and headers on goal. Unfortunately luck wasn't with him on the day, though he continued to contribute over the next few weeks with 'curling corner kicks' that eventually found the waiting feet of his team-mate McLachlan in the 14 April match against Nottingham Forest.

By the end of April, James had scored his tenth goal to climb to third on the list of goalscorers despite only making 25 appearances. Unfortunately he failed to score again for the rest of the season. In the last game, a 1-1 draw at Old Trafford against Swansea Town on 6 May, James made 'perfect passes' that were cleverly masked, but three opportunities were cut down unfairly without penalties being awarded. At one point, a threatening cut in on goal would certainly have found the back of the net if the shot hadn't been stopped by Dewar's back. James still managed to take a corner that found Hine, after every United player in the box had a piece of the ball at one moment or another, for his assist of the season. The 1932/33 campaign ended with Manchester United in sixth place, not high enough for promotion from the Second Division.

A Second Season in Manchester

ON 16 September, Manchester United defeated Brentford 4-3 before 35,000 spectators, beating them at Griffin Park – a feat that had not been achieved by any club since the middle of the previous season. Frame scored for United from 25 yards out with a free kick, and James recorded an assist as he lobbed a ball over the shoulder of his team-mate, Hine, who turned and volleyed it with a quick swing into the back of the net. Brown was in fine form, making ground quickly on the right wing and intuitively knowing how it would be to his advantage to 'thrust in' and shoot while the defence was concerned instead with Dewar and Hine. He scored two splendid goals and led United to a sound and convincing victory. United seemed to gain more and more confidence, but then Fletcher and Holliday struck for Brentford. Brown 'showed a clean pair of heels' to the Brentford defenders and secured the victory.

The following week against Burnley, James scored in a 5-2 win. He showed signs of the 'fulfilment of the promise of a year ago' but wasn't used enough by his team-mate Frame. At times in the dressing room, or on the bus or train, James would take a lot of heat about coming from America. His team-mates would pick on him by talking about Al Capone and other unseemly aspects of the United States, and that would send him into a lecture about what the US was and was not. Inevitably, at some point it would no longer be one on one as three or four guys ganged up against him, but James never let up. The bright side was that James played solidly and was on the winning side again, so a bit of positive jabbing here and there must have helped once in a while. His nickname in the team was 'Sure-Fire' – which surely had a double meaning, given the following exchange.

In one comment in the *Manchester Guardian* about the 7 October match against Preston North End, the columnist described James as seeming to be just a spectator on the field who lacked initiative, often standing by and 'admiring' his team-mates instead of running into the centre and taking the pass that was so blatantly expected. The article read, 'Brown is an enigma; for half an hour he will play really well, then for five minutes he might never have been on a football pitch before. He managed to shoot grotesquely wide when he almost had his nose inside the net.'

At this moment in Manchester, the Brown family was starting to grow. Mary Ann gave birth to the Browns' first child, James Alexander Cormack Brown, at home on 3 November 1933. The family lived at the time at 117 Cromwell Road in Stretford. Eight days later, United played Southampton and the editor included a note in the official programme for baby Brown. How nice it was of the team to send best wishes – as well as a subtle nudge of encouragement for a 'great game' to James senior. They said they were even thinking of starting a United nursery team so the youngster could lace up in no time.

On 18 November against Blackpool, Jimmy scored as United went down 3-1. The *Daily Telegraph* wrote that Brown, at outside-right, was back in the line-up against Blackpool after recovering from an injury. The 2 December match against Port Vale resulted in a 3-2 win for United and was regarded as the best of the season so far against a team previously unbeaten at home. Jimmy finished a rebound from a shot by Dewar and 'smashed it' into the net. Dewar had collided with the Port Vale goalkeeper, Todd, and they fell to the ground, so Brown had a gaping net all to himself. Brown and Black played determined football on each wing, constantly threatening the Vale defenders. 'United owed most to Brown, Black and an unpolished but resolute defence,' the *Manchester Guardian* wrote. The *Manchester Evening News* went one further, headlining its coverage 'Brown Scores for United'.

On 15 December, 'The Captain's Sporting Gossip' column in the *Manchester Evening News* wrote about Brown's goals for United. The columnist contended that, even as criticised as James was, regarding his performance there were few wingers who could show a better goals-per-game average – at that time he had scored 15 goals in 34 games. This all came about during a 'friendly argument' about Brown's worth with the director of another club.

Another long column appeared the following day in the *Manchester Evening News* with the provocative headline 'What Has Brown Done for United?' The article went to great lengths to explain James's success rate and 'valuable goals' based on the different inside attacking partners he had since he returned to the senior side. In five matches played, James scored three goals in two out of the three matches won by United. After his initial run of good form, James missed four matches because of illness. When he returned to the pitch, he scored in each of United's two victories over the next four matches. Over the nine matches he had appeared in to that point of the campaign – alongside five different partners – James put five goals in the net. On the same day the column appeared, United played Swansea Town. James started the match but missed a chance when he nailed a shot that went over the bar. It was a day of missed opportunities all round as Swansea prevailed 2-1.

James started 1934 on a high note for Manchester United as he scored a first-minute goal against Lincoln City on 6 January to 'put a cheer into the hearts of the United team'. The cheer lasted for the first 35 minutes, anyway, as the rest of the game turned into a 5-1 defeat. The *Edinburgh Evening News* announced on 12 January that James, the other three Scots on the team, and five other team-mates were put on the transfer list. Manager Scott Duncan spent more than £9,000 over two years on Scottish players. Duncan felt betrayed that such lists were made public and felt that other clubs were violating privacy and confidentiality laws. That created great surprise in UK football circles. In the aftermath of the news, United's FA Cup third round match on 13 January against Portsmouth was broadcast on national radio in Scotland from Old Trafford.

United drew 1-1 at home against Portsmouth, and the two sides squared off once again four days later in the replay at Fratton Park. Things went worse for United this time around as they fell 4-1 and were out of the FA Cup. The 'only thrill' in Portsmouth's goalmouth was when Brown cut inwards from the right and sent in a terrific cross. It was controlled by his team-mate and Brown ran in to belt it, but Portsmouth's goalkeeper got his fingers on it before Brown could finish. There were over 18,000 spectators at the match, producing gate receipts of £1,200.

James was back with Manchester United's reserves for their Valentine's Day contest against Burnley's reserves, which ended in a 0-0 draw. United had the better of the opening exchanges. Brown and Ainsworth were nippy but found defender Wallace to be a formidable obstacle.

Brown family in Troon, circa 1925
(Top L to R), John, James, Andrew; (Below L to R), Sadie, mother: Isabella Bell Brown, Jenny and Tom bottom
Credit: James Brown Family Collection

Isabella 'Bella' Brown
Credit: James Brown Family Collection

James Brown, Sr. during WWI, was a decorated balloonist
Credit: James Brown Family Collection

James Brown, left, circa 1928 with Port Chester
Credit: James Brown Family Collection

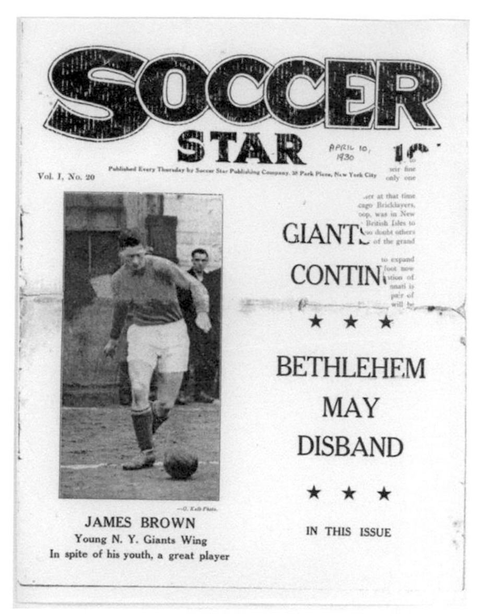
SOCCER STAR

APRIL 10, 1930

Vol. I, No. 20

Published Every Thursday by Soccer Star Publishing Company, 38 Park Place, New York City

GIANTS CONTIN

★ ★ ★

BETHLEHEM MAY DISBAND

★ ★ ★

IN THIS ISSUE

JAMES BROWN
Young N. Y. Giants Wing
In spite of his youth, a great player

Young James Brown on the cover of Soccer Star *magazine, playing for the New York Giants (New York, 10 April 1930).*
Credit: James Brown Family Collection

1930 World Cup individual photo of James Brown in Montevideo, Uruguay (July 1930)
Credit: James Brown Family Collection

1930 US men's national soccer team photo in Brazil, Inaugural FIFA 1930 World Cup.
J. Brown sitting on ground, left side.
Credit: James Brown Family Collection

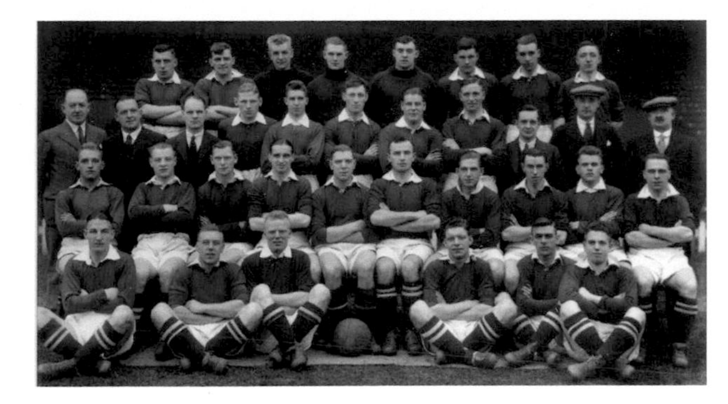

1932 Manchester United team photo. (James Brown, second row from the bottom, third from the left) Credit: James Brown Family Collection

James 'Jimmy' Brown (left) and Thomas Frame, Manchester United's new recruits on trial, 1 August 1932

Brentford FC team photo, J. Brown, top row, far right. 1935/1936 Season (News Chronicle) Credit: James Brown Family Collection

Tottenham Hotspur's player profile of James Brown during the 1936/1937 season
Credit: James Brown Family Collection

Tottenham Hotspur 1936 official programme featuring James Brown
Credit: James Brown Family Collection

Guildford City FC's 1938 Southern League championship team photo (J. Brown to right of goalie)
Credit: James Brown Family Collection

John Bell Brown in action during the early years with Clyde FC after displacing Willie Stevenson 1935/1936
Credit: Gordon Brown Family Collection

Cartoon and caricatures of John Brown with Clyde FC
Credit: James Brown Family Collection

No. 7.

J. BROWN

(Clyde, Goalkeeper)

Standing 6 ft. and scaling 12 st. 1 lb., John is one of the best built keepers in Scotland. Born and bred in Glasgow, he previously played for Shawfield Juniors and was a Scottish Junior international against England, 1935. Snapped by Clyde and instantly made a "hit." Ousted the then "regular" goalie, "Willie" Stevenson, from the League side. Possessor of a "safe as houses" clutch, his uncanny anticipation enables him to fake the hardest of shots without effort. Is a "scratch" man at golf.

Topical Times Photo

SCOTTISH
SERIES
ISSUED BY
JOHN SINCLAIR LTD
NEWCASTLE-ON-TYNE

Topical Times *card of John Brown in the 'Well Known Footballers' with Clyde FC 1939*
Credit: James Brown Family Collection

1939 Scottish FA Cup Final programme, Clyde v Motherwell
Credit: Peter Brown Family Collection

John Brown posing with Scottish FA Cup after Clyde's victory over Motherwell on 24 April 1939
Credit: Gordon Brown Family Collection

Brown brothers in Troon early 1930s (L to R) Andrew, James, John and Tom kneeling
Credit: James Brown Family Collection

Jimmy Brown (ball over his head), George with dog, Pal, and mother, Mary relaxing at the beach in Troon circa 1940 Credit: James Brown Family Collection

John Brown in goal with Scottish Football League (1) against English Football League (3) on 2 November 1938. Team photo before the game at Molineux, Wolverhampton

Tom Brown, Commando in the Army during WWII
Credit: James Brown Family Collection

Brown Brothers during WWII in Troon (L to R - Andrew, James, Tom, John) in early 1940s
Credit: James Brown Family Collection

Tom Brown, policing the penalty area as goalie for Ipswich Town v West Ham United during the third round of the FA Cup in January 1950
Credit: James Brown Family Collection

Teenager George Brown enjoying a half-time orange during a soccer match in Connecticut
Credit: James Brown Family Collection

George and James before Greenport United match
Credit: James Brown Family Collection

United almost took the lead with a typical Brown corner that swerved its way underneath the crossbar – but Burnley's goalkeeper, Conway, was fortunate to turn it away in the nick of time. On 5 March James played in another draw for United's reserves against Sheffield Wednesday's second team. It was a scrappy but fitting 2-2 result as neither team could gain the advantage. James scored before the interval to put United ahead 1-0. Frame had given him a clear course towards goal with a long pass. He 'dashed off at top speed' and gave the Sheffield goalkeeper no chance to save the blast on goal. Overall, United were the more impressive side but were unable to muster a third goal to claim victory.

James was back with the first team on 7 April for the league match against Bradford City. He was particularly effective, earning one penalty but failing to secure another two minutes later; though James was again taken down in the penalty box 'in another raid' on goal, United's appeals for justice fell on deaf ears. James shifted to the centre-forward position, doing moderately well during his short time in this spot.

One week later against Port Vale, James had an average game. Though he looked a bit clumsy in the centre of the attack, he still scored from a chance that couldn't be missed and was as 'leggy as a colt' as United secured a much-needed 2-0 home victory. The 21 April contest against Notts County ended in a 0-0 draw. At this point in the season, United were fighting to keep their heads above water and out of relegation danger. A draw was better than a loss, as Millwall could have used a defeat to their advantage to climb up the table. United played well, and Brown, who had been limping early on in the match, was 'a keen leader'.

On 5 May, the final matchday of the 1933/34 season, United found themselves in 21st place in the 22-team Second

Division. Lincoln City were already guaranteed to drop to the Third Division. With 32 points from 13 wins and six draws, United were one point away from safety. Their last game was against Millwall, the team just one point above them in the table. A draw or a loss would not be enough to avoid relegation; only a win would allow them to leapfrog the London team. United played 'like their lives depended on it' as Cape and Manley each struck goals to send Millwall down to the Third Division, although James was not involved in the squad.

He was at Old Trafford the following day as United's reserves squared off against Manchester City for the Manchester Senior Cup. In front of a crowd of 5,000 spectators, James scored the lone goal in the second half of a 1-0 victory. He had at least two other 'excellent chances' to score from close range, as did Black. The goal itself was 'delightful', coming after a long dribble down the pitch. Before that, however, James had played a largely disappointing game with several poor scoring attempts. Something clicked after the goal, and James helped lead United as a stronger team for the rest of the match. It would prove to be his last match for the club.

Brown had featured in 16 matches over the course of the season and scored seven goals. Despite the low number of appearances, he still finished as United's second-highest scorer after Neil Dewar, who notched eight goals in 21 matches. Sometimes in any given team there are maybe five forwards at best competing for a spot in the starting line-up. Manchester United's 1933/34 squad featured 18 forwards.

As gifted a player as James was, his determination to get players the equal rights and the decent pay they deserved didn't work in his favour when it came time to scale down the list of forwards. For the first team, James had scored ten goals in 25 appearances during the 1932/33 season. Management frowned upon these equal rights initiatives and relegated him to the reserves during most of 1933/34. If there were 'official' class levels in the UK, players would have been placed at the lowest tier and snubbed by management. You could never, as a player, or talk to anyone in the upper management. Objectively speaking, just reading over reporters' comments from both seasons, you would say that James was quite effective and equally skilful as a playmaker as he was a goalscorer. There was little justification beyond his labour activism for the club to bury him in the reserves.

Maybe one of those other forwards was just better than James over time. There were certainly moments when he was reported to have an average or even non-existent game when he did get into the first team – but, given the relegation battle that United found themselves in during 1933/34, James seemed to struggle no more than anyone else in the team. Over 80 per cent of his appearances featured some sort of positive contribution, either assisting others' goals or putting them in the net himself. The other appearances were negative, bewildering or just plain old average. In his 40 matches over two seasons with United, his 17 goals represented the club's second-highest total.

Three Lean Years in London

THEN 23 years old, James stayed in the reserve team at Manchester United until 24 May 1934, when he was sold to Brentford for £300. James received an accrued share of £25 in the transfer. With the new season around the corner, James played in a six-a-side tournament benefiting the Jubilee Fund on 24 August at White City. Brentford started off the 1934/35 season in the Second Division, and James was in their reserves. On 20 September James was part of the squad that drew 1-1 against Bristol City's reserves. His 'fine work' as a winger led to an assist for Brentford's goal. The rematch a week later saw Brentford win 3-0, winding up 'two points to the good'. Brown scored the final goal with a brilliant shot.

Brentford's 8 October match against the Metropolitan Police ended in a well-deserved 2-0 win at Griffin Park. The Brentford half-backs supported the forwards' efforts and helped secure a goal in the first half. Then Brown scored a 'somewhat lucky' goal at the end to seal the result. Over 3,000 spectators attended the following day as Brentford's first team took down Tottenham Hotspur in a 3-1 win. Spurs were a man short for over 70 minutes due to a bad shoulder injury suffered by Clarke. That made attacking from midfield and then building up from the flanks a lot easier for Brentford, whose right-wing pair of Brown and Robson combined well as they interchanged positions often and created havoc. After

Tottenham held out at 1-1 for a long time, Allen and Brown scored to win the game for Brentford.

Two weeks later Brentford played Clapton Orient. The *Daily Telegraph* writer said that Clapton fought 'pluckily' and did their best to keep the score down. Brentford's midfield kept up the pressure and, until suffering an injury, Sullivan was their most dangerous forward. He scored the first two goals in the space of a few minutes, and Brown finished off Clapton with a 'clever dribble' and a strong finish for the third goal. Brown proved to be 'a lively winger' in the second round of the London Challenge Cup, a 0-0 draw against Fulham at Griffin Park on 23 October. Brentford played well considering that their centre-half, Scott, collided with a team-mate and damaged his nose before the end of the first half. Robson made some clever touches and both sides did well enough to deserve a replay the following Monday.

The 30 October replay at Craven Cottage proved a strong battle, with Brentford coming away with a 3-1 victory and the right to meet Chelsea in the semi-finals. Gibbons and Brown 'shone on the wings' and led a smart, keen attack. Thompkins, the Fulham centre-half, was responsible for the lapses that caused the first two goals. James swept in, cutting from the right and into the heart of the penalty box, to fire in the third and decisive goal for Brentford. In the semi-final against Chelsea on 12 November, Brentford were the better side in a scrappy match that saw them score two goals without reply. McAloon opened the way with the first after a scramble in the penalty box 15 minutes from full time. Brown secured Brentford's ticket to the London Challenge Cup Final with a 'capital' header. Brentford proved the better-balanced and more forceful side.

Though he often shone for the reserves, it took more than a season before James appeared for the first team. Brentford went from the Second Division to the First Division at the end of the 1934/35 season without James getting into a single match. Even though he made an impact in Brentford's 2-1 defeat on 23 November 1935 against Chelsea at Stamford Bridge, it proved the only game that James would play for the first team. Introduced to top-level football for the first time, James scooped up a nice long pass down the middle and beat the captain, Craig, in a 'very handy fashion'. His shot was as good as you could have got from a centre-forward. Described as a 'young and tall, heavily built fair-haired reserve, with a nice turn of speed' in the post-match coverage, James fired his shot into the goalkeeper, who fumbled it. There was a scuffle just outside the box and Brown stumbled over Craig's foot – but the referee saw it as Craig tripping him, so a penalty was awarded. Robson converted from the spot for Brentford's only goal in the defeat.

In the Chelsea match, Brown slotted into the centre-forward position. Though the attack was the weak link, Brown looked dangerous when fed the ball properly, which was a rare occurrence. He did have one chance when his team-mate James sent a long ball that Brown ran on to. When he finally got into position to shoot, he ended up hitting the ball directly into the goalkeeper Woodley's hands. Over 50,000 spectators witnessed a great battle and surely got their money's worth. Brentford ultimately lost but not without a strong battle of hard running, chasing and tackling.

By the halfway point and the Boxing Day break, Brentford had spent enormous amounts of money on new player acquisitions. For all that outlay, they were at the bottom of the First Division table along with Aston Villa. The feeling was that Brentford's style of play advanced too fast. In the Second and Third Divisions they relied on pace and that got them to the First Division. But when that pace slackened, because of the style of football at the top level, Brentford didn't have the essential skill and teamcraft to fall back on. There is a limit to which you can play first-class football. When exceeded, the ball gets banged around and runs loose into the opposition's possession. Scottish teams don't often make this mistake; they want to 'keep' the ball. Some said then that if you put a Scot into an English side, he might be bewildered by the pace of the ball because he was not accustomed to playing with team-mates who didn't use the same methods as him.

On 31 January 1936, after their 5-1 win over Northampton Town's reserves in the London Combination Challenge Cup, the *Northampton Mercury* contended that Brentford's reserves would probably defeat many Third Division teams. With the reserves again on 13 April against Portsmouth, Brown 'sent a long punt' to Sullivan, who cracked a shot at goalkeeper Strong. But he was as robust as his surname throughout the whole match and Portsmouth ran away with a 4-0 win. The *Daily Telegraph* reported on the London Challenge Cup Final against Arsenal, who won their place against Brentford by beating Tottenham Hotspur. Brentford, looking to retain the trophy, struggled with the blistering attacks of Arsenal's right-winger Kirchen. Arsenal went two goals up but then Brown got one back to reduce the deficit. McAloon followed up with the equaliser, but Arsenal surged ahead and took control to secure the Challenge Cup, 4-2. Kirchen ended up with a hat-trick.

While James struggled to get into the first team at Brentford, there were still bright spots both on and off the pitch. The best thing that came from this lean year on the pitch was the birth of his second son, George Cormack Brown. George was born in Ealing, London, on 19 August 1935. All in all, James scored 53 goals in 73 games for the reserves and drew a penalty in his only appearance with the first team. Brentford won the 1934/35 London Challenge Cup on the strength of their reserves, though, and James could look back on two seasons where he had proved his worth to other clubs.

He made two final appearances for Brentford's reserves at the start of the 1936/37 season. James last played for Brentford against Northampton's reserves, in a team performance that included lots of shots on goal; Northampton's goalkeeper, Cave, saved six shots in a period of five minutes. Cave, though, proved incapable of stopping an 'almost impossible to save' scorcher from James that resulted in the only goal of the 1-0 Brentford victory. The crowd were thoroughly entertained by the thrilling duel during the whole match and Brentford were good value for their win.

Tottenham Hotspur recruited James for a £1,000 transfer fee in late September 1936. *The Times* reported on 19 September ahead of the match against Bradford City that Spurs would surely beat their bottom-of-the-table opponent with new inside-left Brown taking the place of Bell.

The predictions proved accurate as Tottenham racked up one of their easiest wins of the season with a 5-1 rout. The Yorkshire side seemed to take it for granted that they would get handily beaten by the Spurs. James tangled up the Bradford defence and was 'the only artist' on the field that day. His height and weight added strength to the front line, as did his great ability to cover long distances with 'raking strides'. His passing was good and his shooting better. His acquisition was thought to have been the piece of the puzzle that Spurs had been missing for quite some time. Johnstone, Bradford's right-back, was no match for Brown and Evans. James reminded one reporter of Jack Elkes, a previous Spurs forward who made over 200 appearances for the club. According to Norman Giller of the Spurs Writers' Club, the appearance against Bradford made James the first of 25 players to feature for the first-team squads at both Manchester United and Tottenham Hotspur.

The *Ballymena Observer* noted on 2 October that reserve players were being given more favourable consideration than in previous seasons. The acquisition of Brown was seen as an important 'modern' change in Spurs' management policy – bringing 'weight and power' to their combination. The previous season's injuries were caused by 'win at any price' tactics, where the fear of relegation was on the mind of all team managers. Yet Jimmy played for the first team in only three more matches, all away from White Hart Lane: losses against Barnsley on 26 September and Swansea Town on 24 October, and the 1-1 draw with Aston Villa on 7 November. In the last of his four appearances, Spurs equalised against Aston Villa as Brown and Hall created some 'neat movements' to allow team-mate Morrison to open the scoring.

In a reserve team game against Portsmouth on 16 October, Brown's efforts were hailed as 'genius'. He showed real promise in scoring the equaliser with a relatively simple shot that was missed by the goalkeeper. Later on in the match, with a solo effort, he scored a 'brilliant winning goal' after a great drive that spurred an ovation from the crowd. 'Sometimes a player makes a reputation by scoring a simple goal,' a report declared after the match. Although his reputation earned a few opportunities with the first team, Brown mostly remained with the reserves. On 27 November, James scored one of Tottenham's goals against Southend's reserves in a resounding 9-0 thrashing witnessed by a crowd of 6,162. Against Watford at the beginning of December, Spurs' reserves won 3-1 and James scored two of the goals. The press noted that he 'moved into the centre-forward position and played far better than at inside-left'. Tottenham fielded a strong reserve team again when they played against Swansea on 11 December, and James was busy from the off. He got the first goal in the first five minutes after two previous missed chances. It was again noted that his natural position seemed to be centre-forward. A crowd of 4,655 saw the match and the reserves were up to 11th in the Combination table.

These small successes were not enough to save Brown from the economic realities of the sport. Between 20 and 23 April 1937, James and five other team-mates were officially 'not retained' by Tottenham. He simply failed to show the same level of promise he displayed with Brentford's reserves. His exit was expected to 'cause a good deal of comment' as there were more rumblings about Brown's players' rights activism. This mixed with the frustration of dealing with a non-approving and inflexible management as he bounced between the first team and the reserves during his seasons at Brentford and Tottenham. Though he made only four appearances and scored no goals for Spurs' first team, James scored 21 goals with the reserves in 26 games in the 1936/37 season.

Glory Days at Guildford City

IN THE summer of 1937, James came to an agreement with the management of Guildford City, a non-league club. The two seasons James dominated in attack for Guildford made a mark on the club that lasts to this day. Over the course of 150 appearances, James scored 148 goals – a return that remains a club record into the 21st century.[7] He twice scored four goals in a match and added three hat-tricks over the course of the 1937/38 season.

Brown's scoring prowess helped Guildford City win their first Southern League title in his first season with the club. In the following season he scored an amazing seven goals in one Southern League game against Exeter City – six of which were headers. This set another club record for the most goals in one match, which remains in place as of 2022. Chris Pegman, the acting chairman of Guildford City, said, 'Jim Brown is regarded as one of the best, if not THE best player ever to pull on a Guildford City shirt.' The club failed to defend their Southern League title in the 1938/39 season, however, as they finished as runners-up by a single point to Colchester United.

In September 1937, Guildford felt that they had undoubtedly secured the finest forward line since the club

7 This tally includes a combination of Southern League senior and midweek matches, trials and friendlies.

was founded in 1921. The new recruit led the line brilliantly using his height, weight, and powerful shot with telling effect against Norwich City's reserves on 28 August; Guildford walked over their opponents in a 9-3 rout. One week later, again against Norwich, James was acknowledged with most of the credit for outwitting the defence with clever ball play, crowning his effort with a successful shot.

James was always referred to as 'Brown (J.)' by the club because of the presence of another forward with the same surname, Dick Brown, or 'Brown (R.)'. These two men came to be known as the 'Brown Brothers' despite the lack of blood relation, with a synergetic reading of the game and deft anticipation of each other's moves.

On 16 September, Guildford beat Bath City 3-0. Bath needed almost the whole first half to settle down and compose themselves but were never a threat. The second half was much calmer and attacks against Guildford were more frequent and exciting. Forward George Bytheway helped them take the lead, and essentially disintegrated the Bath attack. Ten minutes from the end, Bytheway nailed another goal and James added one for good luck.

Against Colchester on 18 September, Guildford must have regretted that Leslie, their former team-mate, was against them instead of with them. Colchester's stalwart 'third-back' pivot was meeting old colleagues from Guildford – and took great delight in stopping them. James, starting at centre-forward, simply could not shake him off. Brown, however, also missed a 'sitter' when he received the ball while unmarked and shot wildly past Ritchie, who went to tackle him, and Colchester won 5-0. A late-October tilt against Tunbridge Wells Rangers saw Guildford valiantly battle in vain, suffering a 3-0 loss. Early on, James raced on to a pass from Dick Brown and sent in a 'scorching shot' which seemed certain to settle in the back of the net. Rangers' goalkeeper, W. Beale, made a 'gallant dive across' to turn the ball away. Guildford did little for most of the game, with Rangers defender Nsindy shadowing James so well that he didn't have a good look at the ball before the final whistle.

Guildford shook off a second straight 3-0 loss, this one coming against Bath City, by securing a cathartic 4-3 win against Bristol Rovers' reserves on 8 November. Rovers were dealt a huge blow in the first minutes of the match when their outside-right, Long, collided with Guildford's Foulkes and fractured his collarbone. City capitalised on this right away, attacking with 'a series of raids'. Guildford posted three quick goals, with James working his way through the defence and tapping past Ellis for one. In the second half, Rovers fought back to level the score, but with five minutes to go James headed the winning goal. It was later singled out as the most thrilling game of the season.

On 13 November 1937, Guildford proved too formidable an opponent as they hosted Cowes at Joseph's Road in the fourth qualifying round of the FA Cup. It's always funny to read an opposing fanbase's justification for games their team has lost. Guildford won 3-0, and as soon as the final whistle sounded Yachtsmen fans and writers pointed out that it was the 13th match of the season for the club – and also the 13th day of the month.

By half-time there had been no goals. For the first time that season, Guildford had failed to score in their favourite goal. In the second half, Cowes were thoroughly outclassed and outplayed. Blanchard, the Cowes goalkeeper, kept James from joining his team-mates on the scoresheet but Guildford were still into the next round. The one shot that James managed to fire in flew past the wrong side of the post. Blanchard had collided with his upright and had James enjoyed a bit more time to line up his shot he would have scored the easiest goal of the match.

On 27 November, James was again Guildford's 'live-wire' leader as he scored with a grand shot, delivering Reading a knock-out blow in the first round. The success was thoroughly merited. Around Christmas James then notched a hat-trick against Folkestone. Not every one of his shots landed in the net, however; near the end of a game against Plymouth Argyle's reserves in late December, Jimmy hit a 'real pile driver' that struck the opposing defender and 'laid him out'.

The first match of 1938 ended in a 2-2 draw with Plymouth. In a game that went back and forth until the final quarter of an hour, James equalised to earn Guildford a share of the points. A 25 February game against Rangers demonstrated City's ever-rising confidence and the team's ability to come back from severe odds, as they fought from two goals down to win 4-2. Guildford had also come back from a two-goal deficit in the second half of their previous game against Newport County's reserves and pulled away for an astonishing 7-2 win.

When Guildford faced Colchester on 2 April, Brown impacted the final result despite being closely guarded just as he had been in almost every other match through the latter half of the season. Ten minutes from the end, and trailing 2-1, Jimmy sent the ball into his team-mate Bytheway for a crushing equaliser. Then, just four minutes from time, Brown recorded the winner rather luckily with a swerving shot which deflected through the advancing Smith and past the otherwise well-positioned goalkeeper. Guildford were quickly becoming known as 'notoriously good second-half winners'.

The *Western Morning News* reported on 18 April about the 2-1 win over Torquay United's reserves in which James scored the winning goal with a smart, low drive in the 37th minute. Brown thought he had scored again in the second half but it was disallowed because of an offside ruling. He had always played high up the pitch, risking numerous offside calls during his career, and this time was no different.

Another match reported on in the same edition was the victory over Cheltenham. Guildford's front line were pressed to attack after losing the previous meeting, coming out quickly from the first whistle. James notched an assist, heading on an Ives corner for Bytheway to crash into the back of the net. James got a quick goal of his own to help put Guildford further ahead and helped them secure a 3-1 margin by half-time.

Guildford took the Southern League championship on 7 May 1938 by securing victory against Swindon's reserves. The winning goal came from an individual effort by James when he broke through the centre of Swindon's defence and appeared to be tripped up by a defender, though he didn't fall. The referee awarded a penalty and, though Swindon protested, the decision stood. Dick Brown took the penalty and put Guildford ahead. In fact James hadn't been tripped, but from where the referee stood it appeared to be a clear trip at the edge of the penalty box. James had missed two penalties in the previous match, so it's no wonder that the other member of the 'Brown Brothers' stepped up to the spot.

James ended the season with 38 goals out of 94 scored by Guildford – accounting for 40 per cent of the team's total – in 38 appearances, at a goal-a-game pace. The team's closest goalscorer was McPheat with 15. Over the course of the year, James had ten one-goal games; five games with a brace; three hat-trick performances; and a pair of four-goal outings. He also scored one goal in the FA Cup.

Milestones and Near Misses

ONE OF the earliest games of the new 1938/39 season saw the defending Southern League champions win 3-2 against Yeovil & Petters United on 2 September. Guildford strengthened their side with the summer acquisitions of Charles Calladine, the former captain at Blackburn Rovers; Tom Sillett, the former captain of Southampton; and William McPhillips, a former Scottish international. James headed in Guildford's second goal against Yeovil.

A hat-trick for James dealt Bath City their first loss of the season as Guildford ran away with a 4-0 result. On 10 September against Swindon Town's reserves, Brown again came out strong with a powerful close-range header to score inside the first two minutes. He completed his hat-trick against Swindon and was greeted with a rousing cheer from the crowd. In another attempt, Jimmy headed past the goalkeeper, Bryan, but was reportedly penalised for jumping – an odd citation for sure. Three minutes before the half-time whistle, James headed another goal. Swindon protested because they felt he was offside. This time, however, the call went in his favour.

In another meeting against Swindon's reserves on 1 October, James assisted the first goal after feeding the ball out to the right to McPheat, who then scored with a powerful shot. Bytheway worked the ball into the goalmouth towards

James, who headed a 'picture goal'. A crowd of 1,927 attended the match and the club collected £40 15s 9d at the gate. On 10 October, James nailed another hat-trick against Torquay United in a 7-0 thrashing. By 28 October Guildford were still blasting through the first half of the season undefeated and maintained their streak with a 1-1 thriller of a match against Tunbridge Wells. Though James had 'wreaked havoc on most Southern League defences' he couldn't shake his shadow, Ainsworth, who neutralised him completely. By the latter stages of the second half, James finally broke through the defence unchallenged and bore down on goal. Before he could shoot, however, Rangers' goalkeeper Mittell threw himself at his feet to prevent what seemed to have been a certain goal.

On 20 November Guildford again met Swindon's reserves, with Brown bursting out of the starting blocks and taking advantage of a defensive lapse to run through and force a corner. Guildford weren't able to finish. A free kick from halfway gave James a chance with a strong header, but Swindon's goalkeeper Bryan leapt up and managed to pull down the ball. Bryan was unable to hold on to it, with Tole pouncing and scoring a fine goal. Brown kept up the pressure, eventually putting the visitors on level terms. Bryan got his revenge against Brown, making a point-blank save that thrilled the crowd. Jimmy then 'cleverly' worked an opening for a team-mate which was narrowly missed.

There used to be a supporters' column called 'On Dit' – French for 'We Say' – in the *Surrey Advertiser*. It would cover Guildford's games, players or opponents. One supporter said that Guildford made Swindon look too slow for a funeral. The column also noted that James Brown came from a family of footballers, and went on to mention that his brother John played for Clyde and his other brother Tom, not yet 18, was going to play for Ipswich Town. The supporters wished the young Tom well. They also suggested that James had been in a hurry to get away to London to meet Tom since his signing. During the 1938/39 season, James played against Ipswich Town's first team. Tom was moving up in the ranks at Ipswich, but he was still in the reserves and did not get the chance to play against his older brother.

Aldershot dealt Guildford a deadly blow, eking out a 4-3 FA Cup first round replay win on 30 November in front of 9,000 spectators. The 'Brown Brothers' fought valiantly, with James making two 'gallant attempts' and finally coming away with a goal and Dick scoring twice. The dressing rooms offered two distinct atmospheres: Aldershot's players laughed and chatted about the match while sipping hot tea, and Guildford's heroes changed in silence.

The 10 December 1938 showdown against Exeter City's reserves marked the crowning moment of James's already staggering goal-poaching season. The popular centre-forward played smartly on a rain-soaked and mud-sodden pitch, using his head to put six goals past the keeper as well as one with his boot. Each goal was enthusiastically applauded and, when he walked off the field after the match, he was bombarded with pats on the back and plaudits. The seven goals broke the club record for the most in a match, though James was quick to acknowledge his team-mates' support. In the 'On Dit' column after the match, supporters quipped that the Exeter net was baptised eight times and offered 'Hats off' to Jimmy for the fine entertainment of his marksmanship. As another new year came to a close and Jimmy celebrated his 30th birthday, Guildford City boasted a success rate of just two losses in 20 games.

Four days after the calendar flipped to 1939, Guildford took on Worcester City in a key league game. Both teams were unbeaten on their home turf, and that didn't change as Worcester took home no points after their visit to Surrey. Guildford pulled off a lucky draw when Worcester's midfielder Kirk failed to clear a corner with his head – and it landed in the back of the net. The *Surrey Advertiser* noted 'Jimmy Brown's Fine Effort' to break away by himself on a 35-yard dribble and let loose a 'powerful cross-drive' that the goalkeeper barely managed to gather up, much to Brown's sure dismay.

Arsenal took their reserves to Guildford on 11 January, and the hosts got off to a thrilling start in the rain as James joined McPheat and Dick Brown with goals in the first five minutes to open an early 3-0 lead. Jimmy's goal came from a corner that he headed towards the target. The ball bounced off the post, but Jimmy collected his own rebound and finished into the back of the net. Jimmy assisted McPheat's goal minutes later. Both clubs were equal, at the top of the Southern League standings, and only goal ratio separated the two teams. The Bisley Boys' School Band played courageously before and during the interval. City let the Gunners back into the contest with an own goal followed by a penalty, but then further distanced themselves in the second half. Bytheway and James knocked in 'cleverly headed' goals to make it 5-2. A reporter said after the match that Brown 'flashed it with his head'. Then two minutes later, Brown controlled well on the left wing and crossed for Bytheway, who 'dashed in' and headed swiftly past Arsenal's keeper, Maynard. Later in the second half, Jimmy and his team-mates made a raid on the Arsenal defence. Jimmy looked certain to score, had it not been for Maynard fearlessly collecting the ball from his feet.

The weather continued to yield miserable conditions throughout the winter, but Jimmy 'inspired the attack' match after match as he 'displayed rhythm and cleverness' in the forward line. He was proving especially fearsome with his head – notably with one effort against Chelmsford and three more against Folkestone to close out January. The *Surrey Advertiser* praised Jimmy after the 6 February win over Newport County's reserves for 'his strategy and brilliant headwork'.

Not every result went in favour of Guildford, however, as they fell 4-2 on Valentine's Day against Cardiff City's reserves. Throughout the game Jimmy played clever and purposeful football, and created many dangerous openings. Three minutes before the interval Jimmy drew Guildford level with a great goal, but Cardiff pulled ahead with two more before half-time. Guildford dominated the majority of the second half, but Cardiff were impregnable in defence and finally scored the fourth goal for insurance.

Wednesday, 22 March was a milestone day for Jimmy as he netted his 100th goal in two seasons for Guildford across all competitions, reaching triple digits in the 2-1 win against Dartford. Dartford had only won four matches that season, but Guildford gave in to the old adage that sometimes you can't help but play to the level of your opponent. This was the case in general throughout the match, but it didn't stop Jimmy from scoring. City managed to with a quick raid straight from the kick-off, and it ended when McPheat passed off to Jimmy for an easy tap-in in the opening moments. City got their second goal as Dick Brown converted a header from a free kick then, a few minutes later, Jimmy netted a goal – but the referee had already blown the whistle and the game came to an end.

In late April Jimmy was out of the line-up with a severe bout of tonsillitis in what proved the worst possible moment to become ill. Ipswich Town's reserves were visiting, with his younger brother Tom starting in goal. Though Guildford walked away with a 3-0 win, young Tommy held the line well. Dick Brown sent in a corner that Tommy leapt for, collected and cleared. He also dealt with a surprisingly accurate shot from Calladine at the near post. Tommy continued making 'brilliantly judged saves' even after City knocked in two goals, and in the end the three-goal defeat was not indicative of his valiant efforts against his older brother's club. What a rush it would have been to read about the two siblings battling – one to score and the other to save the day. Alas, just as earlier in the season, the opportunity was not meant to be.

On 6 May, the *Surrey Advertiser* wrote in its 'Sporting Notes' that the City attack was in a weak spot without Jimmy Brown's direction and inspiration. His tonsillitis remained so acute that it was feared he wouldn't play for the remainder of the season. Four days after the column appeared, Brown returned to the line-up and scored twice to help his team win against Folkestone. For the first goal, Robinson took a free kick and found Jimmy, who hesitated because he thought he was offside. When there was no whistle, he continued clear on goal to finish the effort. He then missed another opportunity when he kicked the ball directly against Folkestone's goalkeeper. 'A [quality] goal that convinced everyone' was scored by Jimmy two minutes before the interval. After the tonsillitis scare, though, Jimmy's health issues were not entirely behind him. On 26 July the *Surrey Advertiser* reported that he was again on the sick list and had been X-rayed, as there was a suspicion that he might be suffering from appendicitis.

In a twist of fate, Colchester United beat Ipswich 3-2 in the deciding match of the season. The points from the victory allowed Colchester to take the title away from Guildford. Just as he had against Guildford, young Tommy Brown played a 'fine game' but was unable to secure a win for Ipswich.

This time the result hurt rather than helped Guildford, who failed to defend their championship and ended the season in second place by a single point. Over the course of his 41 Southern League appearances in 1938/39, Jimmy scored 42 of Guildford's 126 goals. The next closest was his 'brother' Dick Brown with 23. In addition to his seven-goal masterpiece against Exeter's reserves, James added four hat-tricks and five braces over the course of the campaign and also scored twice in the FA Cup.

Last Hurrah at Guildford City

TO KICK off the 1939/40 pre-season, Guildford matched up their first team and reserves against each other in a 23 August friendly. It was an opportunity to assess form and showcase new players. One arrival of promise heading into the campaign was the new inside-left forward, Buckingham. The game offered a chance to see how he would fit in with Jimmy Brown's offensive tactics. Jimmy received a 'rousing cheer' when he netted his first goal for the first team, and as he barrelled dominantly through the game he finished his hat-trick with the sixth and seventh goals to complete a good workout.

The first match of the new season took place the following week, as Guildford drubbed Dartford 5-0 on 30 August. Jimmy, 'with a nod here and a deft flick of the foot there', led the front line well. He scored and assisted 'on a brilliant piece of individual work'. Three days later in a friendly against Aldershot, Bytheway, McPheat and Jimmy worked together in perfect harmony. For one goal Jimmy received the ball down the middle, rounded the defender Grant, then cut between the backs before scoring in what was 'a glimpse of Jimmy at his best'. Another comment after the match said that Jimmy was again 'too wily' for Craig in defence thanks to him scoring two of Guildford's five goals.

But 6 September 1939 changed everything for sport in Great Britain. The threat of hostilities had loomed for some time and finally Britain's declaration of war against Germany brought an end to all sports matches across the country – at least for the moment. In that first week of official wartime status, Guildford took a 'spirited visit' to Tunbridge Wells Rangers and produced a five-goal performance thanks to the fantastic forward line efforts of John McPheat, George Bytheway, Dick Brown and especially Jimmy. McPheat opened Guildford's account with a great goal before Jimmy banged in the second goal with his typical effort. Bytheway scored the third, after Jimmy took the ball from City's own half and used his speed to get a clear run. Then he placed it with confidence for Bytheway to finish. Bryn Ives led the advance for the last goal, laying it off to Dick Brown for the finish. On the way down and back, the newcomers in the team enjoyed the rendering of popular songs. Charlie Calladine enjoyed the trip and said the spirit of the team was 'infectious to all who travel with them, for they are a happy and enjoyable set of fellows'. One gentleman from Tunbridge said that City's team played a calibre of football which was truly first-class. This same individual politely mentioned that he sincerely hoped his side wouldn't meet City in the FA Cup further down the road.

A few weeks later, wartime friendlies were permitted so 9 September saw Guildford and Dartford go at it again, Guildford racking up the score even higher than the last time. Because of the 'cries of war' the gate returns were severely diminished, yet 2,228 fans still passed through the turnstiles to watch the 7-0 victory at Joseph's Road. The match started off at a fast pace and Jimmy netted the first goal after 13 minutes from a corner by Dick Brown, sending the ball inside the post and into the net. The opponents's goalkeeper, Jones, did his best to keep Guildford's score down and prevent them from reaching double digits. He smothered a close-range shot from Dick Brown, 'fearlessly' gathered the ball from Jimmy's toes on another attempt and gathered McPheat's chance from a header. Jimmy earned an assist as he put a great ball through to Dick Brown for the sixth goal. Later on, Jimmy and Bytheway closed out the scoring with some 'pretty interchangeable passing' before Bytheway finished.

Guildford came up against Millwall in a 2-2 draw a week later. Jimmy opened the scoring after 18 minutes with a 'clever goal headed sharply to the target' from a Bytheway corner. An opposing defender who worked as a policeman described Jimmy after the match as 'a crafty leader that needed close watching'. In two more September friendlies, both against Crystal Palace, Jimmy smashed in four goals in each outing. With Jimmy also scoring against Tunbridge Wells and Charlton Athletic, Guildford didn't lose their first match of the patched-together season until 25 October, finally being taken down by Jimmy's old club Brentford in a 4-2 defeat.

The month of November 1939 proved vexing for Jimmy on the scoring front. A game against Norwich City's reserves 'caused a laugh' when Jimmy headed too high from a cross that was carefully placed for him. Guildford still won 8-0 but it was 'not a happy game' for Jimmy for, 'strike as he might, he couldn't get a goal'. The following week in an outing against Reading's reserves, he continued to be closely shadowed like he had by them the previous season and was once again thwarted by the goalkeeper. Jimmy had 'a poor match' – not because of any lack of effort, but because no matter what tricks he employed the goalkeeper had a response. Jimmy was again sufficiently shadowed by Ridyard when Guildford won 4-2 against Tunbridge Wells Rangers in the first week of December.

The drought finally ended in the 13 December game against Norwich's reserves, as Jimmy showed 'a welcome return to form' with a well-placed shot past the advancing goalkeeper in a losing effort. His 'spectacular form' continued against Dartford on 20 December as Jimmy knocked in four goals. In one of the programmes before the FA Cup match against Cowes, Guildford listed the leading scorers but also made the point to say that, as great as it was to celebrate a goal, they also had to congratulate the goalkeeper, defenders and midfielders behind the forwards who helped create that goal. That's what teamwork is all about – and it's a shame that this talented team wasn't able to continue.

The turn of the year saw Jimmy helping out the reserves as the first team didn't have many matches in January. City's reserves played on 17 January against Camberley & Yorktown, whose defence was tested by 'the dash and wiles of Jimmy Brown, City's prolific Southern League goalscorer'. They survived the test. Jimmy sent one shot wide, then headed a cross-shot that rolled through the legs of the keeper but crept just outside the post and out for a goal kick. Camberley ended up winning 2-1. Fortunes turned again on Valentine's Day 1940 in a Surrey Senior Cup showdown against Cobham. Guildford were 'toying' with their first-time Surrey Cup opponents, winning 6-0 as Jimmy appeared twice on the score sheet.

Another wartime friendly, against Chelmsford City on 28 February, resulted in a 6-3 loss. Jimmy, 'being a fine leader of the attack', scored all three Guildford goals and would probably have scored more had it not been for a cut to the head that kept him off the pitch for some time.

Guildford's 2-0 win against Dartford on 23 March sent them into the final for the Eastern Section of the Southern League Challenge Cup. The featured battle of the match was the duel between Jimmy and Rosier, whose tackles were quite unorthodox, but his work kept Brown in check. Guildford continued in fine fashion against Woking in the Surrey Cup, winning 3-0 with Jimmy netting two of the goals. Guildford then suffered a 4-3 defeat to Chelmsford in the semi-final of the Southern League Challenge Cup on 10 April. Jimmy wasn't in form and missed a clear opportunity. He did manage to get one goal before the interval and assisted another, but it wasn't enough as Chelmsford found a late winner.

George Bytheway had been away for military duty for a long while, and the 20 April match against Shorts Sports marked his return to the line-up. Bytheway was as match fit as ever and Guildford won 5-2. Jimmy scored the final goal with a header. The 24 April Mayor of Aldershot Cup tie ended up in a thrilling 3-3 draw against Aldershot. Guildford were the holders of the cup and needed to beat Aldershot in the return match. In the first half, Jimmy brought Guildford level with a fine goal right before half-time. Aldershot's defenders seldom let the City forward line get easy passes from the defence, although their goalkeeper made a spectacular save from Jimmy, who saw another header bounce off the foot of the post. He was finally rewarded when he headed in a pass by Calladine. Jimmy put Guildford ahead for the second time in the early moments of the second half, and then sent in another terrific drive that was stopped by the goalkeeper. They forced a few more corners in an attempt to take the lead in the last moments but it was not to be.

The *Daily Mirror* mentioned that Jimmy had been loaned out to Brentford as a centre-forward in what the newspaper called an 'FA League Cup tie' against Fulham on 1 May. In that game Jimmy made some nice combinations with Scott A. James, and often threatened danger, but unfortunately for the Bees it came to naught. Brentford's Rooke fired a shot over the bar, and Brown rallied the home crowd hopes with a well-directed shot that landed in the net to give them the lead. He enhanced his reputation as a goal-getter, but unfortunately Fulham replied with two of their own. In the second half Manley and Brown missed a pair of gilt-edged chances to take the lead, and both forwards were given a talking-to about their keen and persistent attention given to the goalkeeper, Boulton – no doubt trying to force him into the goal along with the ball, as was the custom in those days.

Also on 1 May, City defeated Woking 3-1 to win the Surrey Combination Cup for the second year in a row. Unfortunately, given he was on loan with Brentford, Jimmy wasn't able to celebrate with his team-mates. Heading towards the end of the season, Guildford played an exhibition match against the RAF XI at Joseph's Road on 8 May, with Jimmy scoring twice alongside goals from Buckingham and McPheat in the 4-2 victory. Guildford's 18 May friendly with Southampton produced some entertaining football in front of over 1,000 spectators. Although they were depleted by injuries, the 'Brown Brothers' Dick and Jimmy notched two goals each in the 4-1 win. In the 1 June return against Aldershot for the Mayor of Aldershot Cup, Guildford lost 6-1. Jimmy was injured about ten minutes into the match and changed spots with Dick before following medical advice and sitting out the second half.

That early, hobbled exit was the last time Jimmy appeared in Guildford's stripes. His cartilage injury in June against Aldershot was a confirmation of the worries he felt about the state of his knees. The hastily reorganised 1939/40 season saw Guildford finish as runners-up in the Southern League Eastern Section.

John Bell Brown, Pride of Clyde

JIMMY WAS hardly the only one of the sons born to Isabella and James Brown who went on to excel on the pitch. John Bell Brown – only referred to as 'Jock' in footballing press, never anything but 'John' or 'J.B.' in the family – was born on 21 February 1915 in the family home at North Shore in Troon. Six years younger than Jimmy, it was apparent from an early age that John was gifted with exceptional hand-eye coordination and displayed natural football skills and catching ability. He was born 'a sporting natural'. Due to the money pressures on Isabella, who was saddled with raising her children on her own after her husband left for the United States, John left school when he was just 14 to start an apprenticeship in a riveting gang at Troon Shipyard.

By that point the expanded family lived in a ground-floor flat in the Exchange buildings at the top of Templehill. Isabella ran a small shop to earn a living, supplemented by presents she received for acting as the midwife at many Troon confinements – though she had no formal qualifications, her own experience with eight births, together with her wonderfully caring nature, made her most welcome in all homes and she was called upon regularly by local doctors.

John only lasted 18 months in the shipyard. Since his chores involved constant crawling and lying in the dirty, confined chambers in the ship's lower regions, the resultant heavy toll on his clothing meant their constant replacement costs left little contribution for the family upkeep. He turned to gardening while also attending Auchincruive College, working at the big houses on the outskirts of Troon. During his labours he met Margaret Currie, a shy Troon lass working as a nursery nanny, at Monklands.

Nineteen years old, having finished school but still wanting to play with his buddies, John was heading to the cricket when the rain came and ruled the match off. So he sat at his house, looking out the window at the drizzle, scheming and planning. He went out in the rain to see his buddies and convince them of his intention to start a football team. They all thought it was a great idea, founding Troon Corinthians in 1934 as a way to play football on the weekends. At one point during the club's existence, John was the chairman, secretary, treasurer, trainer and consultant.

Later on that year, he played for a Prestwick Junior League team called Glenburn Rovers. In one match against Auchinleck Talbot, a first-round replay in the 1933/34 Ayrshire Junior Cup, John played in goal. Along with heavy rain came pounding pressure from Talbot. Glenburn won the toss and chose to go against the strong wind that went from goal to goal. As Talbot kept hammering away at Glenburn's defence, John stood tall more than once with 'grand' saves, including just before half-time when he brilliantly tipped the ball over the crossbar. The first half ended scoreless but in the second half, Glenburn's defence greatly improved and Talbot found it harder and harder to get by big Jock Brown. Once Talbot finally found the back of the net seven minutes into the second half they did have further opportunities, although Jock still came through with an amazing save when he flung himself right across the goalmouth and just managed to stop the ball from going over the line. Brown was the answer for the Glenburn side in the replay. It had been a long time since the reporters covering the match had seen such a masterly display in goal as Jock helped lead his team to a 3-1 victory.

John's exploits in goal soon caught the eye of Clyde manager Frank Thompson. Thompson mentored him, giving tips about play and ball handling. John's hobbies were golf and badminton, as well as caring for pigeons and other birds. Badminton, he later said, helped keep him on his toes and trained his eyes on a moving object. In 1934, John played in the Scottish Amateur Golf Championships. He failed to qualify with rounds of 80 and 82. On average, it's not very remarkable – but consider the fact that he had never enjoyed the luxury of owning a full set of clubs before that year.

John also played in the Junior nationals at Tynecastle. Scotland beat Ireland 1-0 with the big Troon fellow standing out head and shoulders above the rest of his comrades. He started his real youth career at Shawfield in 1935, when Thompson signed him after the junior international match between Scotland and Wales. He then started for Clyde later that year. When Jock was a provisional signing for Clyde's Shawfield Juniors, Arsenal's head scout Alex James approached him. Alex stayed with Jock for a week of golfing and sounding out what the young lad planned to do. There were secret talks with Clyde that were denied at the time, but Clyde refused to sell and Jock felt a duty to stay with the Bully Wee. Upon signing full forms with Clyde, Jock got an increase on his £2-a-week pay as a provisional signing.

John's goalkeeping was as controversial and unorthodox as it was ahead of its time. He liked to play off his line and narrow the angle for on-rushing forwards. He won a cap for the Scottish national team against Wales, represented a Scottish league XI against the English league, and was the winner of the 1939 Scottish Cup with Clyde. Jock was always disappointed that he lost a single goal in that cup run as it was a soft penalty awarded in a third-round tie at Ibrox. Had it been Rangers' normal penalty taker Brown would have saved it, because he knew where he liked to place his shots.

John had a 'safe as houses' clutch and made 129 appearances for Clyde between 1935 and 1942. He also signed with Hibernian between 1942 and 1944, though he made no league appearances. From 1944 to 1946, John went to Gillingham and made eight appearances. Returning to Hibernian in 1946, he made a dozen appearances over two seasons with the Scottish league champions. A move to Dundee saw John play 14 more times during the 1948/49 season, and he entered one final league game with Kilmarnock while serving as their physiotherapist and trainer in 1949/50.

Tom Brown, Commando Between the Sticks

THOMAS 'TOM' Brown was born on 26 October 1919 in Troon. Little Tom played golf just like his brothers and followed in John's footsteps as a goalkeeper on the football pitch. Rumours started to circulate on 26 July 1937 that young Tom – who, though still just 17 years old, was even more well-built than his brother John – could be a possible replacement for the departing second Clyde keeper, Stevenson. What a treat it would have been to have two brothers competing for the same spot.

He instead signed for the Glens at the start of the 1938/39 season and was described by the *Cumnock Chronicle* as a 'major sensation'. The secretary of Cumnock Juniors had miscalculated the closing date for retaining players, and as such several of the side were free to join other teams. This included Brown, who signed for Glenafton Athletic – so it seems Tom did have a spell at Cumnock Juniors. By October 1938, his youth career as a goalkeeper had properly started with Glenafton. He played in a trial match against the New Cumnock juvenile side Connel Park Rangers and was quickly signed. His first competitive game was in a 7-3 league win over Dreghorn at Connel Park, New Cumnock (Glens didn't move to their current ground, Loch Park, until 1960).

Although they lost the next league game away to Kilwinning in early August, the Glens then rattled off eight league wins in 23 days. That included a top-of-the-table clash against Auchinleck Talbot at Beechwood. Talbot took an early lead, but the tide turned when Tom saved a penalty and Boyle subsequently bagged a brace for Glens.

Cup games proved less rewarding, as Glens crashed out in the first round of the Scottish Junior Cup after a 4-1 loss at Larkhall Thistle in early September. Tom's name appeared less frequently after this, with 'J. Lee, committee man, put[ting] up a good display between the sticks'. Former Glens keeper Matt McEwan's name also appeared regularly at this point, leading Tom to sign with Ipswich Town in November 1938 for a 'handsome' transfer cheque. At the same time Tom was playing, he had to take up an apprenticeship, like his brothers before him, and he chose painting and decorating.

Tom played for the reserves at Ipswich from 1938 through to 1940, and during the war he was with Ayr United in the 1945/46 season. Tom went into the army in between these stints. He was elected to the elite commando unit that was parachuted into northern China to help guerrilla groups engaged in fighting the Japanese, a story recounted in *Gas Masks for Goal Posts: Football in Britain During the Second World War* by Anton Rippon. After his mission was complete, he waded in shoreline water and camouflaged himself with surrounding weeds and vegetation until a navy ship came and picked him up. His time as a commando was difficult and although he never spoke about it, he was deeply affected.

On 21 March 1940 a Scottish Select XI played against an army team that included Tom Brown between the sticks. With his 'brilliant goalkeeping' the commando held the Select XI to a draw in front of a crowd of 6,000. Five days later, Tom played for Clyde against Third Lanark, in the place of his older brother John, who was called away for military duty. Third Lanark pierced the defence four times in the first half but failed to get the ball past Brown, who made quite an impression, with reports stating that, against a 'less capable' goalkeeper, Lanark might have made the result different. Clyde ended up winning 4-0 in front of a 4,000-strong crowd.

On 6 April 1940, Tom made a one-off appearance for Ayr in a Scottish War Emergency League match against Queen of the South. He was registered with Ipswich at the time, and he travelled to Dumfries from his training quarters 'somewhere in Scotland'. An announcement on 3 May informed that the Scottish divisional team who held the Scottish FA XI to a draw would play Yeovil & Petters United on the following day. Tom, the 'brother of Clyde's international goalkeeper', was named as part of the line-up.

In December 1945, when still registered with Ipswich, he rejoined Ayr while on leave from the Far East. During the 1945/46 season he made nine appearances, all in the league. We can rest assured that his potentially lethal adventures would have left him with no nerves about guarding the Ayr goal in that post-war phase. Tom went back to Ipswich around July 1946 and won the starting position the day after the reserve team beat Crystal Palace on 11 September. *Gas Masks for Goal Posts* mentioned that the regular keeper, Mick Burns, was no longer able to play after having fallen down the trolley bus stairs. Tom's important event of 1946, however, came when he met Nancy Quantrill, who he would marry after just a year of courtship.

After the war ended, Tom played with Ipswich's first team in the Norfolk Jubilee Cup against Norwich City on 24 May 1947. Brown did all he could to hold off Norwich's numerous attacks. After one particular threat, Tom bravely dived in to snatch the ball off the striker's toe and avert a clear chance. Nonetheless, Norwich were 1-0 up by half-time. Norwich livened things up and went straight down the pitch at the start of the second half, with Brown 'throwing himself at a shot' and forcing the striker to put the ball inches wide. Brown made another 'fine save' among a commotion in the penalty box but was unable to stop the subsequent penalty awarded during the melee. The Canaries ended up winning 2-1.

In another Jubilee Cup match the following May, Norwich again beat Ipswich 2-1 in front of a crowd of 7,435 spectators. Reports noted that both goalkeepers made 'fine saves' throughout the contest. Norwich started off with a rush, and Brown saved a shot from Morgan and followed it up by punching out an incoming corner. The two teams played for the Jubilee Cup again the following year, and once again Ipswich fell short in a 1-0 defeat. Tom was 'sound in goal' and his achievements included a save from a penalty.

Ipswich played Chelmsford in a crucial FA Cup match on 13 December 1949. Tom was able to punch down a Chelmsford raid early on, but with nine minutes to go Chelmsford's Hurst sent in a low 'grounder' that beat his sprawling and hopeless dive. In early January 1950 Ipswich took on West Ham United in the third round of the FA Cup. In such a critical showcase, this was not the finest of matches for Tom as Ipswich collapsed 5-1 at the Boleyn Ground. Five minutes into the second half, a West Ham forward ripped a shot from outside the box that 'deceived' Brown on its way into the net – and then, in the space of 12 minutes, two more goals were scored. One had Tom challenging for a 'high dropping' ball that should have merited a free kick for Ipswich. The attendance was 25,000 with receipts of £2,450, a take of about two shillings per person.

During his time with Ipswich, Tom made a total of 116 first-team appearances (111 league matches and five in cups), plus 108 more starts with the reserve team. The height of his career came over the three-season run between 1947 and 1950.

Tom's last match with the first team came in the Third Division against Nottingham Forest on 24 February 1951, Ipswich falling 3-1. Ipswich ended up 17th in the league standings that season. As his career came to a close, Tom played one final season with Bury Town during their 1950/51 campaign. On 30 November, Bury played Arsenal in a 1-1 draw, which saw Tom and his defenders 'brilliantly anticipating' Arsenal's attacks. Tom was 'at peak form' as he continuously rescued Bury from dangerous situations. The pitch was heavy and as the wind whipped around it caused the ball to dip and swerve. Bury's 'Old Timers' were not very happy campers in the conditions. Tom ended his career with Bury in August 1951 and continued painting and decorating as his trade until retirement. He passed away in May 2000 and is survived by his wife Nancy, their children and grandchildren.

Reunited in the Wartime Years

WHEN THE war broke out in 1939, John and Tom Brown went to work as riveters at Troon Shipyard under the management of their uncle, foreman 'Big Tam' or 'Big Andy' Bell. James joined them soon after he completed his season with Guildford City. A local article entitled 'All Together Again' focused its attention especially on John, who had traded in his Clyde uniform for Troon Shipyard riveting clothes. During World War Two, Ailsa built vessels for the navy including several Bangor-class minesweepers. John and his brothers were known as the 'Bell Squad'. One heated the rivets, one held them in the hole, and two of them took turns hammering the rivets in.

After the first day of riveting at the shipyard, James, who had soft hands, came home and chased everyone out of the house and dunked his bloodied hands in a bucket of concentrated salt brine, much like boxers toughened their hands back then. The pain was excruciating, and he didn't want anyone to hear him crying. No matter what, 'religiously' every Sunday, brothers John and Jimmy would head out to play golf – noting that the war had taken 20 yards off John's drive.

As seen in the past during an itinerant professional career that saw James bounce from team to team for the same reasons beyond his playing ability, he was again an outspoken union activist for equal worker rights and equal pay. When he and his brothers worked at Troon Shipyard, they were making only a third to half of the wages paid by the nearest shipyard a few miles away. Troon paid by piecework for each rivet placed. So they resolved to 'down tools', although they were the only group at the shipyard to go on strike. They constructed a large tent with a fire to keep warm and held out until their uncle came in and broke up the strike, firing them. The termination effectively tore up their war exemptions and sent the three brothers into battle.

The second-oldest of the Brown brothers, Andrew Brown, was born in 1913 in Troon and later married Catherine Sinclair. At the outbreak of the war he was an electrical lineman, repairing downed power lines on the street poles in the countryside. His son William used to go with him in the tiny van when he was called out to repair duty during the night. That work exempted Andrew from service during the war. He had already served in the Merchant Marine Navy as a sailor from 1929 to 1935 and sailed for 'Hungry Hogarth' – so called because his ships fed the crew meagre rations.

James was also exempted from wartime service because of a busted eardrum from a childhood mastoiditis infection, and the youngest two brothers avoided the draft by enlisting. Tom served as a commando and John entered the Royal Navy. They were sent out for tours and missions lasting long stretches at times. Tom played in several matches for the Army XI during the war along with appearances for Ayr United.

Well into 1940, when Jock wasn't called into Her Majesty's Royal Navy, he kept shining for Clyde. In a match against East Fife on 4 March, Jock's experience and superb anticipation was in full form as he made a full-length dive to save a fine shot by East Fife's forward Morrison. Brown leapt out on another occasion, catapulting himself at Morrison's drive to deflect it for a corner. A week later Clyde faced Dunfermline, and 'Big Jock' came to the rescue once again. The opponents' attacks were relentless, forcing corner after corner, but Jock was there to keep them out.

On 4 May Jock was in goal for St Mirren against Celtic. It was not unusual to see players go from one team to another during the war, as they often played with the team that was closest to where they were stationed, and Jock bounced between Clyde and St Mirren over the next year. On 26 August he was back with Clyde and was beaten by Falkirk on a fine shot from 30 yards out by Jimmy Fiddes. On 16 September Jock again featured for St Mirren and gave a 'first-class display'. On 21 October Clyde dealt Hearts a 'Sock in the eye!' and the most crushing defeat in the Edinburgh club's league history, a 10-3 pasting. The Bully Wee had that 'sitting on the end of a rainbow' feeling after running rings around their opponents. One month later, Jock's older brother Jimmy joined Clyde and played for the club in February and March of 1941. It must have been an exciting time together, as none of the brothers had ever played in the same team at the same time before.

The war continued to shuffle players around the country as service commitments limited playing time. Jock had been loaned out to Hamilton Academical on occasions during the war, and on 27 November 1942 Hibernian made a successful transfer bid for the goalkeeper. A post-Boxing Day meeting with Rangers a month later saw Jock coming to the rescue as Hibs fought a rather nasty match, and Jock traded acrobatics with Rangers' goalkeeper Jerry Dawson. A disallowed first-half Rangers goal fuelled the already anxious crowd, while Dawson was knocked unconscious by a bottle that gashed the back of his head and forced him to be carried off the field for medical attention. Hibs were up and down, and Jock was there to get them out of the mess, with the two teams sharing the points in a 1-1 draw.

Jock spent ten months at Hibs before receiving his 'calling up' papers and reporting for duty at a naval training base in late September 1943. A *Sunday Times* article noted that Jock had been a riveter and hoped to get a game with a club in the London area. Given the incident at Troon Shipyard a few years earlier, it was interesting that Jock's previous riveting experience was highlighted. Jock still managed to play a few games for Hibernian while on leave from duty, including against both Celtic and Rangers. In November, he also played for Fulham in England against Aldershot while stationed at Chatham for a time during the war.

From Father to Son

BORN IN Ealing in 1935 during his father's time playing for Brentford, George Cormack Brown spent the early years following his parents around Britain – from Brentford to Tottenham to Guildford City and then back to the family's roots in Troon, Scotland. They initially moved in with their grandmother on Logan Drive where he enjoyed the coastal town. There was lots of space to play and create his own world with his older brother James. After the family got their own flat, George never really saw much of his grandmother, especially around holidays or birthdays. The Browns, the Lambies and the Clarks all lived in Troon, but everyone seemed to live their own lives.

Since Troon lies on the west coast of Scotland it has always been notorious for being a cold, windswept town. It consisted of rows of houses and tenements on Temple Hill, Gillies Street, and Barassie Shore along with the sprawling estates on the outer limits of the town. George attended the 'wee school' on Academy Street. The social happenings around the town centred around ice-cream and fish and chips. Around the flat where the Browns lived on Portland Street was the amusement arcade and Mazzoni's ice-cream parlour, which was run by a few Italian families: the Mazzoni, Togneri (Johnny 'Tog'), and Lunardi clans.

The houses on Portland Street had a very large and long back yard that served four or five properties, but there was no back door. So to head out and play in the back yard, George had to climb out of the window or go out of the front door and walk around the corner. The flat was made up of a hallway, living room, a bedroom and kitchen. Mary, James, George and Jimmy slept in the same bed, the boys curled up at the foot. Breakfasts were typically porridge and/or bacon sandwiches and what they called 'dinner' at noon – mince and tatties (minced meat and potatoes) or fried fish. Father James was working as a riveter at Troon Shipyard and Mary worked at various establishments such as the amusement arcade or as an usher at the local movie house.

There were weekly rituals consisting of household duties including washing clothes early on Monday morning, or cleaning the flat as a family on Saturday morning. Mary climbed in and out of the window to hang clothes on the line after boiling the laundry in a large, cast-iron tub under a coal fire at six in the morning. That back window was the gateway and the key to many of the essential household tasks. It was also crucial for young George and his brother Jimmy, as they used it as an escape route to freedom. Those Saturday morning chores saw Mary up at the crack of dawn to go on a 'frantic tear' cleaning the flat. George and Jimmy were expected to help out, but as often as not they slipped out the back yard window to go fishing off the Ballast Bank. Slowly lifting the window up no more than eight inches to keep it from squeaking, they were in the clear with just enough room to shimmy their way out. The boys enjoyed fishing a great deal and would set their sights on bream or saithe. It was worth the thrashing they would get when they got home.

George was bullied at school by a boy named Ramsay. He was in the same year group but was older because he had been held back two years in a row. George went home to complain to his dad but was ordered to resolve it and then come back home when it was settled the right way. A fight was arranged 'in back of the co-op', a place where school fights were settled. Word went around the school and around town like wildfire. With everyone gathered, there was absolutely no way to back down. After much anticipation, the fight was anticlimactic before George got in a lucky punch that bloodied Ramsay's nose and he folded. Jimmy had already been instructed to step in and take care of things if George was in trouble.

When George was a youngster, still just 4ft 4in tall, he went to caddie at Troon Golf Club without telling his dad. One day, his father was cleaning windows at a house that lined the course. He saw his son carrying two full golf bags, and told George to stop and come with him. Stomping off to see the head caddie master, James gave him hell for letting a boy of his age carry such weight. He forbade George from ever caddying there again. James, retired due to injuries sustained over the course of his 13 years as a footballer, worked in various roles after his playing days. Aside from riveting, he took a job briefly as a postman, but then decided to start his own window cleaning business around Troon. He would grab his V-shaped ladder, cleaning accessories and wheelbarrow and clean the windows of the large estates in the area.

During the war, there were few luxuries – no fruit and, as George's parents recalled, horrible cigarettes such as 'pasha', a Turkish offering. This was because of German submarines that would intercept and torpedo supply ships heading towards the UK. Luckily, around 1944, an Argentinean cargo ship made it through with a load of fruit. Each child in Troon was allowed one orange. For whatever reason, Jimmy was not able to get in line. Young George plucked up all his courage and said that his brother couldn't make it and he deserved an orange as well; his courage was rewarded as he received two oranges.

Margaret 'Marilyn' Brown was born into the post-war family on 29 April 1945. Tragically, in 1946, first-born son James contracted tuberculosis, which had generalised over a month and a half, and he never recovered. Mary, his mother, was constantly with him before he passed away, and little James did everything he could to reassure her that everything would be OK and that he was ready to go. He said that there was a woman that was with him and that she said she would accompany him. Just before passing away, Jimmy was in a coma for three days. On the fourth day he awoke and started singing the lyrics to the song 'Beautiful Dreamer' by Stephen Foster. Mary and James had no idea how little Jimmy knew the lyrics and it haunted them until their last days.

Jimmy was only 13 when he passed away at nine in the morning on 26 April 1947 at the family's home on 54 Logan Drive in Troon, and he was buried around Marilyn's first birthday. His father always believed that a new wonder drug, aureomycin, could have saved Jimmy but the family didn't have the money or connections to obtain the medication. Around 1948, the Melody Maids came out with a song called 'The Three Bells'. The song relates three stages of the life of 'Jimmy Brown' (completely unrelated): his birth, his marriage and his death. It was taken from a French song called 'Les Trois Cloches' in 1945, later made popular by Edith Piaf in 1952. Needless to say, when that song came on the radio, there was no way to escape it, and the memories would come pouring back through the family's hearts and minds.

After Jimmy's passing, George was pulled out of school to care for Marilyn so his parents could both work and save enough money to emigrate to the US. In 1948, James and

Mary made the decision to head back to the US to make a new start with George and Marilyn. In preparation for the voyage, the Brown family moved out of their flat in the days before the cruise liner was supposed to dock. Terrible Atlantic storms caused a ten-day delay in the ship's arrival and the family was forced to take up lodging in a one-room flat in a section of North Shore Troon called the Barassie. It was an undesirable area of town, with a slaughterhouse located nearby and raw sewage flowing into the bay. With all their money committed to the trip, the family lived off of puffed wheat and milk. For heat, they fortunately had a relative employed by the railway who would arrange to throw out lumps of coal when passing by the flat. It was great until others caught on – and then the fight for coal would ensue.

Mary and the kids went over first with third-class tickets, arriving in New York on 21 December 1948 aboard the *Queen Elizabeth* cruise liner. James followed a few months later, because of either travel document issues or the money for the voyage. They settled in Greenwich, Connecticut, a considerably wealthy city north of New York. One notable family living there at the time was the Rockefellers. Mary worked at their estate, and little Marilyn used to go there and play with the children in the family. Marilyn even learned how to roller skate on their circular driveway. The Browns chose to settle in Greenwich because a network of extended family members had already established themselves in the area: George Cormack (Mary's brother) was a chauffeur at a wealthy estate, and uncle Syd and aunt Bella worked as the live-in gardener and housekeeper on the castle grounds of the estate of Wallace Groves. He was a prominent financier, associated with Meier Suchowlański – otherwise known as Meyer Lansky, the 'mob's accountant' who worked with Lucky Luciano in the Mafia.

After moving down to the Bahamas, Wallace was credited as a driving force in the growth of the modern Bahamian economy. When James finally arrived in the US, he kept it a secret from the kids. One night, at the Groves estate, George and Marilyn came into the huge living room where there was a fireplace with a big and elegant chair. The chair was facing the fireplace and away from the kids, so when the person in it showed his face – it was none other than their father. The two excited children ran and jumped into his lap, smothering him with kisses and hugs. No doubt he had brought some sweets with him from Scotland, surely distributing them with a whisper to the kids, 'Don't tell Mum!'

At this point George was 13 or 14, and he attended Greenwich High School from 1949 to 1952 – the same school that Truman Capote, the American novelist, screenwriter, playwright and actor, who notably penned *Breakfast at Tiffany's* and *In Cold Blood*, had attended ten years earlier. Like all new international students, George was invited to join the International Club to help him integrate as well as possible and to use that international distinction to bond with other new students.

In late September 1949, columnists Bill Graham and Joe McKeown mentioned a new man on the Hispano roster – James Brown. Joe and James were old pals, and he wrote about how Brown used to 'please the crowd' with his wing runs and crosses with the old New York Giants in the good old days. Joe used to say around town that James was 'the best outside-right in the country'. Hispano manager Duncan Othen heard that James was back on the east coast and wasted no time signing him up.

James had a run with Hispano and proved that he was 'just what the doctor ordered' for the club. There was a story that James used to tell about going back to the US in 1949 and trying to play again. Over the years, he mistakenly said it was with the Philadelphia Nationals, playing outside-right and was up against a young but unskilled full-back, but it was the Brooklyn Hispano. He beat the full-back but the youngster kept recovering and got goalside of him. At half-time, exhausted and sitting on the bench, James was approached by a league official and asked his name. 'Well Brown,' the official replied after James told him, 'I've been watching you carefully. Keep it up. You have a bright future in soccer.' James, 41 years old at the time, appeared in only a couple of matches for Hispano, and he played alongside goalkeeper Gene Olaff, who would end up being a great friend of George later on in life.

Naturally, George turned to playing soccer, and it got off to a rough start. He was still growing and was a lot smaller than the rest of his team-mates. Back in those days, public high school soccer leagues were small and there were only a handful of games in a season. James took a job at the local high school as the varsity coach during the 1951/52 season. That way he could guide George and instruct others at the same time. James taught George how to use his body and low centre of gravity – an advantage of being shorter – to dummy the opponent without fancy footwork.

In one season, the Greenwich High School varsity soccer team went undefeated, with four wins and two draws. They scored ten goals, George accounting for eight of those as he demonstrated 'Scottish know-how' by 'turning in excellent performances against all opposition'. The high school team emerged as county champions. When James got a job coaching varsity soccer and rifle craft at the prestigious private Brunswick School in Greenwich, George shifted over there as well. Famous graduates include actor Peter Fonda;

Cameron and Tyler Winklevoss, the two brothers who first conceived Facebook at Harvard; and other film directors. James stayed at Brunswick as the varsity coach from 1952 until his 1974 retirement.

Greenport United

AFTER HIS aborted time with Hispano, James was a bit restless and wanted to get 'back into the thick of it' on the pitch. On 11 September 1950 he joined with Pat McGarrity, Robert Wilson, James Morris, Pat Gillespie, Sam Donnelly and Tom Doran to form a Greenwich-Port Chester team to compete in the newly revived Connecticut Amateur Soccer League. Just 15 years old at the time, George signed with the newly formed Greenport United team created by his father. On 13 October, Greenport signed three new players; one, full-back Johnson Wilson, had played in Scotland as a member of the Troon Athletic Club in Scotland. The club was recognised as one of the top soccer organisations in Scotland.

During the 1950 season, there were some problems that needed ironing out. James called for a meeting with the league referees concerning the aggressive behaviour of many players. No yellow or red cards were given during this season, so James laid down the law to better control weekend games. The following Sunday James was ejected from a game and suspended for fighting.

Greenport continued their assault with an eye on the top spot in the Westchester division of the German-American Football League by defeating Bedford Hills. George and Ed Touhey were the 'big guns' with one goal apiece in the

2-1 win. It was Greenport's fourth consecutive win in the division. With any assault, though, there are bound to be casualties. Greenport United lost two players, John Bamford and Walter Kuhlman, to knee injuries during the match. But that wasn't all as 'tempers rose and fists flew' during the match. A free-for-all occurred with players and spectators running on to the field. Two players, one from each team, were sent off.

The duo of George (six goals) and Ed Touhey (ten) accounted for the bulk of Greenport's 17 goals scored during the 1950/51 season. Sam Donnelley junior was their only other scorer that year. It was an auspicious start for the new club as they prepared for the season ahead.

On 30 September 1951, Greenport toppled the Bridgeport Americans 7-1 at Byram School Field to get the 1951/52 season off to a great start. The Americans went ahead after 15 minutes, but then James Mooney and Ed Touhey put Greenport in front and they never looked back. Touhey remained the 'big gun' for Greenport. James Brown, a few months away from his 43rd birthday, even chipped in with a goal. The Greenwich squad, Connecticut League champions the year before, showed signs of not letting go of their title for at least one more year.

A month later, Greenport won in the first round of the National Amateur Challenge Cup with a 1-0 victory over Stamford. James Brown, between his duties as manager of Greenwich High School's undefeated team, scored the only goal to advance to the second round against Bridgeport Vasco da Gama. The two sides met on 12 November at Corpus Christi Field in Port Chester. Ed Halley, George Bex and George Brown scored for Greenport to bring the score to 3-3. With seven minutes to play, Greenport goalkeeper Ronnie McAllister blocked a shot but momentarily fumbled the ball and Vasco's Santos pounced on the rebound for the winning goal.

On 22 October Greenport were boosted by a James Brown brace in the 5-2 victory over the New Haven Booters. Bex, John Doherty and Davie Liddle scored the first three goals before Brown added the final two. Greenport eventually lost 3-1 to Stamford in the Connecticut State Challenge Cup. The two clubs met several more times throughout the season, their 19 November showdown ending in a 2-2 draw with George having opened the scoring after around half an hour and Stamford ultimately levelling the game with ten minutes left. Both father and son were playing. On 27 November against the same opponents, George came good with five minutes left to score the Maroons' winning goal with a 'hard shot' that carried Greenport to a 2-1 win.

The 10 December match saw Greenport chalk up their fifth straight victory, against Naugatuck, in a hard-fought 3-2 tussle. The 'popular booter' George knocked in a goal directly from a corner – it looked like the Browns had a knack for that. Then George's team-mate, Davie Liddle, sent him through for his second goal of the day. Father James finished it off with goal number three. It must have been something to watch George at outside-left and James at inside-left, feeding each other, creating space, and both looking to score.

In a thrilling 7-5 win against the New York Hungarians, George scored four times. He starred alongside Ed Touhey as Greenport and the Hungarians traded six goals in the first half, and the two sides were deadlocked at 5-5 when Greenport scored two late goals at Recreation Park, Port Chester for the win. The Greenport squad also beat a strong Eintracht 11 from Long Island in a 4-2 win. George's 'fine, all-around play' allowed Greenport to see off Eintracht, who hadn't been beaten in the previous three years of competition.

The win advanced them to the second round of the Dr Manning Soccer Cup, where the Brown family scored all three goals in a 3-2 victory over the Greek-Americans. The match was played in a river of mud at the newly surfaced Steinway Oval in Astoria, Long Island. James scored the first goal, and then it was son George who equalised and put Greenport ahead in a downpour that lasted throughout the match. Young George 'was the whole show' in the second half as Greenport advanced to the third round of the cup.

In an 11-2 victory, Greenport ran riot against the Yonkers Sports Club at Recreation Park. George, the former Greenwich High School star 'booter', was again the leading scorer with four goals. That win moved them into the semi-final of the Westchester Soccer Cup.

'Mighty Mite' George Brown scored a hat-trick to help Greenport to a 'great triumph' over White Plains at Byram School Field. 'Brown had a great day' for Greenport, scoring two long-range goals in the first half with the wind at his back. In the second half, he scored a third with the wind coming full force against him. David 'Davie' Liddle followed up with a fourth goal to secure the match. With this win, Greenport felt confident that they could beat the Bridgeport Tigers to the Connecticut state championship.

On 20 November, in a rough game against New Haven Club, Greenport were 2-0 up for nearly the entire match until New Haven levelled the scores in the last 15 minutes. George showed the veterans some 'sparkling play' by scoring both Greenport goals, and even with the draw they remained in first place. On 26 November the Bridgeport Italians were toppled 2-1. It was their fourth Connecticut Amateur League win of the season with one draw. Locked at 1-1, George scored the all-important goal after beating three Italians. Their opponents were unable to score again past James

Brown, who was on goalkeeping duties, the first known instance of him jumping in goal.

While the records are patchy for this period, George scored around 18 to 24 goals, if not more, for Greenport during the season. News then emerged that Greenport, along with 12 other teams, were going to pull out of the Connecticut Amateur League they helped create in order to establish a Westchester County Soccer League.

George Spreads His Wings

AFTER SHOWING so much promise with Greenport, the New York Americans took an interest in George. Joe McKeown, who wrote the well-known 'Soccer Games and Gossip' column for the *Irish Advocate*, wrote on 4 October 1952 that a 17-year-old named George Brown was being looked at by the Americans. He scored two 'good goals' in each half of a trial match and Joe wished him the best of luck. McKeown went on to say that George wasn't ready to fill James's shoes but had good prospects. The player profiles from the same New York Americans trial match talked about George possibly being a 'sensation' with his 'tricky plays and shooting ability'.

Three months later, McKeown wrote that he ran into 'the old New York Giants soccer wizard' James Brown along with his wife Mary and daughter Marilyn as they watched George play for the Brooklyn German-Hungarians. Asking what the family had been up to, Marilyn took advantage of the opportunity to mention that the Browns were reviving the Round Hill Highland Games in Connecticut. Nothing beats free (and such adorable) publicity, and on 11 July over 15,000 people took part in festivities including sporting events, dancing and piping. James split with the group years later and formed Scottish Enterprises, Inc. with George, who served as president. They held the games at the Blind Brook Polo Club in Purchase, New York, for several years.

McKeown also reported at this time on rumours that James would manage the Hungarians. On 29 April, Greenport released George so he could spread his wings. The New York Americans, though, felt that George was too small and released him. The New York German-Hungarians quickly came knocking at his door in 1953 and their manager Nick Muller signed him at the age of 18.

On 24 August, the Knitters (as the German-Hungarians were nicknamed) showcased some new 'luminaries' including Lefty Bryndza, Joe Maca, Robert Kratzer and George Brown. At this time they featured some of the greatest players known to the game. Included in their talented squad were John Souza, Walter Bahr and Joe Maca – three members of the US national team's historic 1-0 victory over England in the 1950 FIFA World Cup, who were all later inducted into the National Soccer Hall of Fame. The German-Hungarians won the warm-up match 3-2 in a charity benefit for the injured Johnny Hild.

On 28 December 1953 the German-Hungarians were knocked out of the National Challenge Cup at Sterling Oval 1-0 by Brookhattan-Galicia. George was selected to play for the German-American Soccer League All-Stars against an All-Star aggregation from the New Jersey State Soccer Football Association in the annual New Year's Day match at Metropolitan Oval in Maspeth.

The German-Hungarians won three consecutive league titles, and even among all the concentrated talent on the roster George earned the league's 1953/54 Most Valuable Player award. The *New York Times* reported on 5 April 1954 that the NY Americans, who released George the year before, were pummelled 6-0 by the German-Hungarians.

George was surely happy to have contributed a goal to that thumping.

At this point in the season, the German-Hungarians were first in the Lewis Cup standings after their first-round win against the Americans. On 17 May the Knitters won the German-American Soccer League (GASL) Big 12 Division with a 2-1 victory over Newark at Farcher's Grove in Union, New Jersey. Up until this Farcher's Grove game, Eintracht were the leaders, with a one-point edge over the German-Hungarians. Eintracht had already completed their fixtures, so the German-Hungarians regained the title they lost the year before with the win. In the deciding Newark game, George scored two goals in the first ten minutes.

In an 11 November article during the 1954/55 season, respected Brooklyn *Daily Eagle* columnist Bill Graham noted that a certain young right-winger from the Ridgewood German-Hungarian team scored a hat-trick in the club's four-goal victory that Sunday. Like father, like son. On 28 March 1955 George helped push the score to 2-0 as Ridgewood beat the New York Hungarians. Two weeks later, on 13 April, Ridgewood listed notable players John Souza, Peter Wiggins, Matty Junger and George Brown as participants for a match against the GASL All-Stars. Briefly, in 1955, George returned to his alma mater and coached them to a county championship. In an exhibition match against touring French side Sochaux on 6 June, George put away the only goal for the GASL All-Star side in a 4-1 loss, beating goalkeeper Remetter to a cross from Gene Grabowski of Elizabeth in the 12th minute.

George was later naturalised as an American citizen on 28 October 1955. As his proven scoring ability was now widely recognised, the New York Americans tried to sign him – but he never forgot the 'you're too small' dismissal from two years earlier and refused to join them. The newspapers *Staats Zeitung* and the *Sports Herald* often created short profiles on players under a column called 'We Introduce'. George was unanimously selected as the 'best player of the year' within his team. The column spoke of the class and influence that James Brown passed along and nurtured in his son by reviving the Connecticut State Soccer League and forming Greenport United and lacing up once again so that he could teach young George on the field. It was a unique experience that helped George appreciate the game and learn the tips and tricks from the 'old New York Giants wizard'. At the end of the column, they spoke of George as an 'excellent footballer and fine fellow'.

Having gained considerable knowledge, confidence and experience playing with the German-Hungarians, it was time for George to move on. He would never forget the generosity and camaraderie within the team. Moving from Ridgewood to Elizabeth, George signed with the Polish Falcons for the 1956/57 season on 15 February 1956. The *New York Times* reported on 25 March that the Falcons won a lopsided match 9-0 against the Baltimore Rockets, with George striking yet another hat-trick and team-mate John Gaidos scoring four. Another *New York Times* article on 6 May reported on the Falcons' 3-2 victory over the Newark Portuguese, with George scoring in the first half of the American Soccer League Lewis Cup tie. James took over as coach between 1956 and 1958. The German-Hungarians also won the 1956 New York State Cup.

On 12 May, 30,000 turned out to see the touring Israeli Hapoel team beat the ASL All-Stars 6-4 at Ebbets Field. The crowd was treated to a pre-game guest appearance by Marilyn Monroe, who attended the match to support the Israeli side with her husband, the American playwright

Arthur Miller. After being driven into the stadium in a convertible, Monroe went out to the centre circle and passed some time in front of photographers who snapped shots of her kicking a few soccer balls. More star power appeared at Ebbets Field in the form of beloved performer Sammy Davis Jr, who provided the half-time entertainment.

In the match itself, the Israelis had already scored five goals to the All-Stars' one by the time Davis came out to perform. In the second half, Ed Moares – the goalkeeper from the Newark Portuguese team – replaced Notari for the All-Stars. The All-Stars showed considerable improvement and George cut the lead to 5-3 with an angled shot after a feed from Monsen. Though the All-Star squad lost, it's likely that the dressing room conversation had more to do with Marilyn Monroe than anything else.

The Polish Falcons beat the ASL champions, Hakoah, 4-2 on 31 May at Zerega Oval in the Bronx, with George scoring along with Gene Grabowski. George scored again in the 4-3 victory against Brookhattan-Galicia to put the Polish Falcons level for first place with the Philadelphia Uhriks. They were scheduled to play the Uhriks a week later for the championship title. Unfortunately, during the 1956/57 season, George tore his anterior cruciate ligament in his left knee. Regardless of this huge setback, he was the leading scorer with 13 goals.

The Polish Falcons opened the next season with George as 'one of the ASL's outstanding players' as he hoped to continue on the heels of the prior season's goalscoring tear. The 8 October match against Brookhattan-Galicia saw George score and the Falcons win 3-1. Against the Baltimore Rockets, George scored three times from the wing position, notching the Falcons' fourth, fifth and seventh goals in the crushing 9-0 win. In another match against the Brooklyn

Italians, George tallied a hat-trick in the first half – a rough way to welcome the new Brooklyn club to the big leagues in its first game.

A Second-Generation American International

FOLLOWING SEVERAL strong seasons at multiple clubs after his departure from Greenport United, 21-year-old George was further recognised for his achievements on the field with his selection to the US national team squad for a World Cup qualifying match against Mexico on 7 April 1957. The blue-eyed 158lb lad, who had been kicking a ball around since he was two years old in Troon, told the *Greenwich Times* prior to leaving for Mexico that the chance to represent the United States 'will be my greatest thrill'.

After arriving at the airport in Mexico City, the US team met supporters who travelled across the border to attend the game. They also encountered the press on the tarmac as they disembarked from the plane. Celebrity radio announcer Escapato met with the Americans along with members of the Mexican Soccer Federation. They stayed at the Del Prado Hotel, one of the most beautiful and most expensive hotels in Mexico.

Once they were settled in and had grabbed a bite to eat in the hotel restaurant, George, Walter Bahr and Gene Grabowski ditched O'Toole, their chaperone, and headed out to check out the Mexico City nightlife. The young lads mingled with the locals, who seemed to know very little

English. 'Two drinks, please!' Not too long after one in the morning the gang returned to the comforts of their beds and it was lights out by quarter past. The next day, it was rise and shine by 8.30am, as they headed down to grab a nice breakfast and read the local sports newspapers to see pictures of themselves on the front cover.

Then it was off to the stadium, where the pitch was in perfect condition. Over 80,000 people were expected to attend. The team had the honour of meeting the recently retired Mexican football star Horacio Casarín, who took time to meet and greet and shake hands with all who asked. After a workout and some sightseeing, George ate filet mignon steak with his room-mate Gene Grabowski before settling in just before the 11pm curfew.

When they woke the next morning, a perfect day awaited in Mexico City. After the opening ceremony and national anthems, the match got under way at the Estadio Olímpico Universitario. Mexico quickly took the score to 3-0 by half-time. Altitude played a big part in the lack of stamina that the US team exhibited – after making a hard run up the field, the Americans could not catch their breath for at least five minutes.

Altitude was not the only reason for the mismatch between the two sides. The Mexican team had been training together for months, and their unity and anticipation showed on the pitch. Though the US had a few excellent chances, the end result was a 6-0 rout. Mexico went on to become the North American representatives at the 1958 World Cup in Sweden, while the Americans would have to wait another three decades before they returned to the sport's biggest tournament.

Though the Americans played three more matches in regional qualifying through July 1957, George was left out of the squad. His start at the Estadio Olímpico Universitario proved his only cap for the United States. He was also in the squad that took third place in the third annual Pan-American Games, held in Chicago in 1959, but wasn't able to contribute much due to a knee injury.

Greenport United team photo in early 1950s. Father James (top, far right) standing over son, George
Credit: James Brown Family Collection

James lacing George up before Greenport United match
Credit: James Brown Family Collection

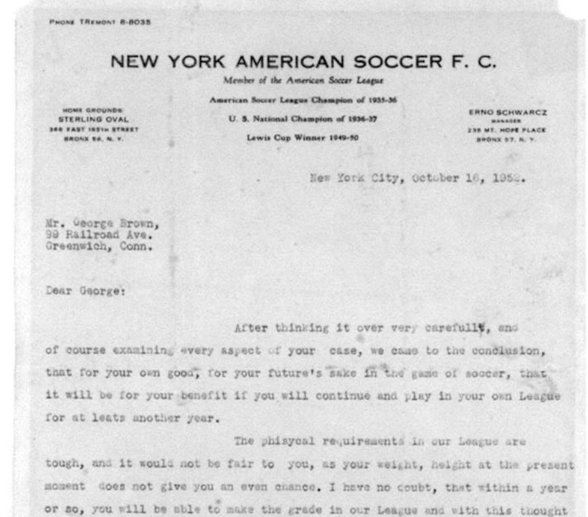

PHONE TREMONT 8-8035

NEW YORK AMERICAN SOCCER F. C.

Member of the American Soccer League

American Soccer League Champion of 1935-36

U. S. National Champion of 1936-37

Lewis Cup Winner 1949-50

HOME GROUNDS
STERLING OVAL
366 EAST 165TH STREET
BRONX 56, N. Y.

ERNO SCHWARCZ
MANAGER
235 MT. HOPE PLACE
BRONX 57, N. Y.

New York City, October 16, 1952.

Mr. George Brown,
99 Railroad Ave.
Greenwich, Conn.

Dear George:

After thinking it over very carefully, and of course examining every aspect of your case, we came to the conclusion, that for your own good, for your future's sake in the game of soccer, that it will be for your benefit if you will continue and play in your own League for at leats another year.

The phisycal requirements in our League are tough, and it would not be fair to you, as your weight, height at the present moment does not give you an even chance. I have no doubt, that within a year or so, you will be able to make the grade in our League and with this thought in mind we decided to send you your release in order, that you can play the game every Sunday. It would serve no purpose for you, being as a young player to stay as a reserve player with us. I am sure that you do understand it.

With the best wishes, and either I will get in touch with you or you can drop me a few lines later on.

Kind regards to your parents.

Very truly yours

Erno Schwarcz, Mgr.

THE UNIVERSAL SPORT SOCCER

Former 1920s Hakoah star, Erno Schwarcz, manager of NY American Soccer FC official release letter to George Brown on 16 October 1952
Credit: James Brown Family Collection

George Brown (7) battling for powerhouse Ridgewood German-Hungarian team at Eintracht Oval
Credit: James Brown Family Collection

George Brown playing with the Polish Falcons of Elizabeth scoring against Newark Portuguese on 6 May 1957, in Lewis Cup competition
Credit: James Brown Family Collection

Marilyn Monroe kicks the ceremonial soccer ball before ASL All-Stars team match against Israel's Hapoel Tel Aviv team on 16 May 1957 at the Ebbets Field Stadium in Brooklyn, New York

George Brown scoring with ASL All-Stars team match v Israel's Hapoel Tel Aviv on 16 May 1957 at the Ebbets Field Stadium in Brooklyn, New York
Credit: James Brown Family Collection

US Men's National team photo at University Stadium, Mexico April 7, 1957 (George, bottom far left kneeling)
Credit: James Brown Family Collection

'Coach' Brown with the Ingonish girls' high school soccer team after winning the Provincial 'A' title on 6 November 1993
Credit: James Brown Family Collection

National Soccer Hall of Fame (Oneonta) historians Colin Jose (L) and Roger Allaway (R) with George Brown
Credit: James Brown Family Collection

National Soccer Hall of Fame (Oneonta) 2007 induction ceremony. President, George Brown proudly posing with USWNT legends and World Cup champions, Julie Foudy and Mia Hamm.
Credit: James Brown Family Collection

The lethal combination! Margaret 'Peg' Brown, National Soccer Hall of Fame (Oneonta) archive manager posing in 2007 with dear friend, Colin Jose, US soccer historian
Credit: James Brown Family Collection

1930 USMNT World Cup team-mates, James Brown & Arnie Oliver sit and talk with George Brown at the first annual National Soccer Hall of Fame induction ceremony in 1986
Credit: James Brown Family Collection

David Brown playing on the men's soccer team at Drew University in New Jersey
Credit: James Brown Family Collection

Jim Brown playing against Westfield on the Scotch Plains-Fanwood varsity soccer team in 1989
Credit: James Brown Family Collection

Alex 'Sanny' Lambie, captain of Partick Thistle in the late 1920s.
Credit: James Brown Family Collection

Gala captain, Peter Brown with the Sevens Cup 1972
Credit: Peter Brown Family Collection

1971 Scotland rugby team celebrate winning centenary match against England. Gordon holding up the bottle with his toe and Peter, tallest to the right with a big smile.
Credit: Peter Brown Family Collection

1971 Scotland v England centenary match at Murrayfield. His Royal Highness Prince Charles, Prince of Wales being introduced by Scottish captain, Peter Brown to Gordon Brown before the match
Credit: Peter Brown Family Collection

Brown brothers at post-match function in kilts
Credit: Peter Brown Family Collection

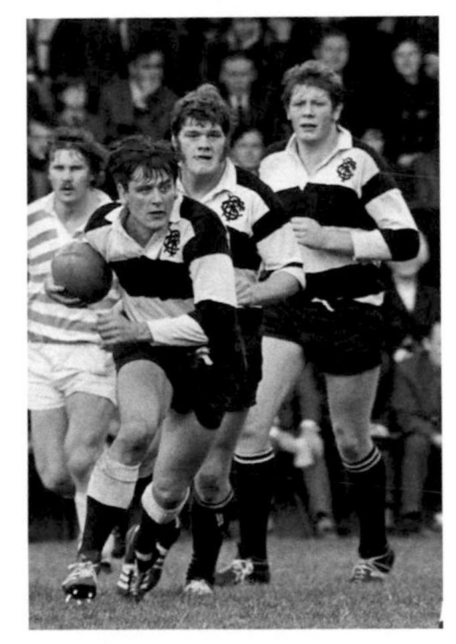

Peter Brown (Barbarians) on the ball, with Fran Cotton (centre) and Gordon Brown at Grange Road, marking the centenary of Cambridge University's rugby club. 25 October1972

Peter Brown (L) and Walter Spangehro after Scotland vs France (16-13) during the Five Nations Tournament on 13 January 1973 at the Parc des Princes Stadium, in Paris.

Gordon Brown in line-out training during the 1974 South Africa British & Irish Lions tour
Credit: Gordon Brown Family Collection

'For a golfer, he wasn't a bad rugby player.' Gary Player hitting the links in South Africa with Gordon Brown in 1974
Credit: Gordon Brown Family Collection

Memorial service programme at Gordon Brown's funeral in Troon in 2001
Credit: Gordon Brown Family Collection

Scotland's Alastair McHarg celebrates the Five Nations Championship with Peter Brown (#8) and G. Brown after Scotland's victory over England, 16-15, in the 1971 Calcutta Cup at Twickenham. Scotland's first victory at Twickenham since 1938. 20 March 1971

Pat Lambie of South Africa in action during the international match against Italy at the Stadio Olimpico on 19 November 2016 in Rome, Italy.

Pat Lambie of South Africa kicks a penalty during the 2015 Rugby World Cup semi final match between South Africa and New Zealand at Twickenham Stadium on 24 October 2015 in London.

Patrick Lambie celebrates after scoring the match winning penalty during the Rugby Championship match between the South African Springboks and New Zealand All Blacks at Ellis Park Stadium on 4 October 2014 in Johannesburg, South Africa.

Western Province wing Bryan Habana congratulates Patrick Lambie from the Sharks after the Absa Currie Cup Final match between the Sharks and Vodacom Western Province at Absa Stadium on 30 October 2010 in Durban, South Africa.

Springbok fullback Patrick Lambie (C) vies with Fiji's center Gaby Lovobalavu (left) during the 2011 Rugby World Cup Pool D match Fiji vs South Africa at Wellington Regional Stadium on 17 September 17 2011.

Patrick Lambie of the Sharks in action during the round two Super Rugby match between the Brumbies and the Sharks at GIO Stadium on 4 March 2017 in Canberra, Australia.

James Brown meeting soccer legend, Pelé in 1976 in Rye, NY during a Pepsi-sponsored event
James Brown Family Collection

Nic and Caz Lambie enjoying a glorious day
Credit: Lambie Family Collection

The Lambie Family - Pat, Sam, Kate and Jack (L to R) Credit: Lambie Family Collection

Three generations representing the Rovers Rugby Club in Durban, South Africa – Nicholas Labuschagne, Sr Pat Lambie and father, Ian Lambie (L to R)
Credit: Lambie Family Collection

Returning to the Falcons

ON 31 May 1957 the Polish Falcons defeated Hakoah 4-2, with George and Gene Grabowski each notching a pair of goals. The Falcons finished the year second in the league, in large part thanks to the scoring prowess of the two men who had recently represented the United States in Mexico.

The close of the season brought another big opportunity on the pitch away from home for George.

On 17 July the headline of the *Daily Herald* in Scotland read 'Yank Sweats it Out at Celtic Park'. While holidaying in Scotland, George accepted an invitation from Celtic manager Jimmy McGrory to train with the team during pre-season at Parkhead. While Celtic were in the US on tour a few months earlier, United States Soccer Football Association president Jimmy McGuire had mentioned to his former club that George would be returning to Scotland during the close-season for a holiday, prompting McGrory to extend the invite. George had already been drafted into the army, so he could not pass up the chance to work out with the famous Glaswegian side while in Scotland. Unfortunately for George, there was no ball play – just physical conditioning, such as a 12-mile run that left him 'sagging at the knees' according to the *Scottish Daily Mail.* After lunch, trainer Willie Johnstone ordered up another six miles. Brown was 'astounded ... but liked it'.

At the start of the 1957/58 season, the Polish Falcons travelled up to battle Fall River at their home stadium on 14 October. This was the first time in 25 years that a team from Fall River – a city known for a previous generation of greats such as 1930 World Cup stars Billy Gonsalves and Bert Patenaude – had represented the Spindle in the ASL. The Falcons were faster, smoother and superior technically to their Fall River counterparts. George scored both goals in the 2-0 win, picking up right where he left off after finishing the previous season with 15 goals to lead the league in scoring. He starred against Fall River despite recovering from a broken right hand suffered earlier in the new campaign, though he pulled a muscle behind his right knee after the second goal in the victory; that knee injury was likely the beginning of the cruciate ligament problems that ultimately led to George's retirement. In attendance for the landmark return of a Fall River club were Jimmy Brown and Bert Patenaude, the two former 1930 World Cup team-mates. They reminisced the day before about days long gone – how great would it have been to be a fly on the wall at that moment? George got to share good laughs with his former German-Hungarian team-mate and Fall River opponent, John Souza.

The following summer, Jimmy Brown – still managing the Polish Falcons – was in the crowd along with Mary and their daughter Marilyn for a six-a-side tournament on 2 July in which George featured for the Yonkers side. Once the 1958/59 campaign got under way, George and the Falcons paid a visit to the Philadelphia Uhrik Truckers on 3 November. George scored five goals, and it was a good job he did as the final score was 7-6 to the Falcons. By 27 December, however, the Polish Falcons were forced to forfeit to Hoboken, citing the loss of a player to injuries and George being drafted to the US Army. While attending Finance

School at Fort Benjamin Harrison in Indiana as a private in the army, George became acquainted with members of the Chicago Red Lions soccer team. He competed in the western finals of the National Amateur Cup with the Red Lions and helped the team finish third in the league with 14 wins and four losses. After training in Indiana, George was based at Fort McClellan in Alabama where he worked in the post finance office.

By 1959, both James and George had left the Polish Falcons. The first signs of the separation came when Bob Allison, a strong, imposing centre-half for the Polish Falcons, was injured in a September 1959 match at Ironbound Stadium but didn't say anything. James asked him if he could keep going on and he said no, so the manager substituted him. In that match, George hit a bullet-like shot – but the ball got stuck on the goal line, covered in mud, and the Falcons were beaten. Later on James commented, 'It was harder to miss the goal than hit it!'

Days later, the Falcons' senior management called James in to talk about his decision to substitute Allison. Because of the substitution all the club's sponsors started pulling their support, arguing incorrectly that Bob had never asked to leave the pitch. The club started to question James's tactics and choices, prompting him to get out of his seat and, albeit in harsher terms, tell them to 'go stuff it'. *The Advocate* reported in its 'Soccer Games and Gossip' column that John McCurley of the Kearny Scots replaced Jimmy.

Once George and James left, the Falcons generally finished around fifth or sixth in the league over the next nine seasons. Only once, in the 1960/61 season, did the team manage to finish as high as second.

Life Out of the Army

WHEN GEORGE Brown left the army, he decided to study at the University of Bridgeport in Connecticut. He was awarded a soccer scholarship, but because of his professional soccer status he was ineligible to play for the university powerhouse. That freed him to play part-time instead for the Elizabeth Falcons. To help pay for tuition, he also coached the university's freshman soccer and varsity tennis teams from 1960 to 1964. In 1961, at Ironbound Stadium in Newark, George played for the Newark Falcons and scored a hat-trick. Joe McKeown said that George 'started the fireworks' when he blasted two goals into the net in the second half. Newark went on to win 7-1.

Father and son were at it again, reestablishing the Highland Games as a festival for Scottish athletic contests, piping and dancing. George also became more seriously involved with Margaret Freese during the early 1960s. Born on 8 November 1938 in Kingston, NY, Margaret – known as Peg – had started dating George in 1958 after they met while she was in nursing school at the Greenwich Hospital. She was friends with George's cousin, Sheila Cormack, who was in her class at the nursing school from which Peg graduated in June 1959. George and Peg married on 2 June 1962 at the First Methodist Church in Bridgeport, Connecticut. During George's university years, the Brown family started to grow. Sharon Ruth Brown was born on 19 December 1963 in Greenwich, and David Alexander Brown joined the family on 31 March 1965.

In his professional career, George was employed by Exxon as a human resources manager. He was sent throughout the world by the company: to Libya during Colonel Gaddafi's *coup d'état*, to Egypt, to Saudi Arabia, and finally settling in Scotch Plains, New Jersey to work at Exxon's headquarters in New York until his early retirement in the late 1980s.

George then went on to run for and win a two-year term on the city council of Scotch Plains-Fanwood. During the 1991 election campaign, James Brown was asked about his son's playing ability. 'He was fast and difficult to stop,' James told the reporter, 'but what most people didn't fully appreciate was his desire to succeed and his willingness to work hard to reach his objective. It's a matter of heart, dedication and commitment. He showed it in the soccer arena, and he'll show it in the political arena.'

Around this time James and Mary, after having lived in Greenwich during most of their lives in the United States and well into their retirement, moved down to Linden, New Jersey, to be closer to their grandchildren and great-grandchildren. They eventually resided at a nursing home in Berkeley Heights, where they shared a room until their final days.

In 1986, James was inducted into the National Soccer Hall of Fame, with George following in his footsteps nine years later. They are the only father and son combination inducted into the Hall of Fame as players. Both were also inducted into the Connecticut and New England Soccer Halls of Fame. At the Connecticut Soccer Hall of Fame induction ceremony in 2000, George accepted his father's posthumous award. A friend of James, George Boyton, said of the elder Brown, 'He was a gifted player, and you had to be phenomenally tough in those days. He knew very surely that he was one of the finest players of his era. He never had to tell you, nor would he, which is so unlike players today. He was a quiet, modest man.'

The Ingonish Years

AFTER COMPLETING his term on the city council, George and Peg moved away from Scotch Plains in 1993 after 15 years in the community. They relocated to Nova Scotia, where they ran Sleepy Hollow Cottages in the town of Ingonish on Cape Breton Island. The couple had also purchased Ingonish Island just off the Cape Breton coast after returning from Libya and taking a much-needed holiday. They headed north to Canada, ending up in Ingonish. On a whim they asked if the island that they were staring at out the window of an Ingonish restaurant was for sale, and as luck would have it they soon owned the place.

Once they relocated to Ingonish, George coached the local girls' high school soccer team and helped lead them to the 1993 provincial championship. The Ingonish high school had fewer than 300 students in all. Despite the small pool of potential talent, Ingonish – with George as coach, an inexperienced goalkeeper, and an injured team leader – ended up winning the Provincial A title on 6 November 1993 after a two-day tournament. Brown described the girls as 'tough as nails' on the playing field. Co-captain Samantha MacKinnon was so dedicated to winning that she went for weeks on end with cracked ribs and never told anyone until after the school won the championship.

Heather Murray, a freshman defender in the Cabot team from 1993, recalled that her first impression of George was that he was 'a bit loud and brash by Canadian standards' during his first training session with the team. Acknowledging that he was faced with a mixed bag of players with a wide range of skills and knowledge about the game on that first day, Murray said that George 'drilled us in the basics during our twice-weekly practices and did an amazing job of teaching us team strategy' and 'quickly brought a new order to our group'.

David Rasmussen, a teacher at the high school who served as the soccer team's assistant coach and whose daughters played for the team, recalled his time working alongside George:

'I will always remember the first gathering we had with George and the team. It must have been at the soccer field in Ingonish. George addressed the group of reticent girls. He did not hold back! He introduced himself by saying that soccer was his life, and he knew the game and was willing to share his knowledge with them IF they were willing to commit themselves to his rules and standards. His name was "Mr Brown, NOT George". They could call him "Coach" if they preferred. I think from that moment on he was "Coach" or "Coach Brown". Later when the girls met Peg she became "Mrs Coach".

'He said that his job was to coach, and he knew his business. He did not need their help with that. Their job was to commit to taking their training seriously and to follow his instructions. They were to show up for practice prepared to work and to give 100 per cent of their ability all of the time. If anyone had an issue with him, his instructions, or their condition on any particular day, they could talk to him privately and in confidence. He would respect them, and they would respect him. George made it clear that his time was valuable, and he did not have any of it to waste. They were to be on time for every event and ready to go to work. I don't think the girls had ever been talked to like that before. Their reaction was, "WOW. This guy is serious!"

'In the third season we won the Nova Scotia provincial championship. George loved winning as much as the girls. As we got to know the opposing teams his game strategies became very intricate. By this time George knew the strength, and weaknesses of every player and was able to use that to deceive and out-fox the opposing coaches. I loved watching him at work. I admired him tremendously because of the seriousness with which he took the game and the respect he showed for the girls that played their best for him. My girls recall that they were impressed by the fact that Coach worked every girl into every game. Some were not on the field for long, but they played and felt part of the team.'

Throughout all of George's coaching career, he insisted that coaching this team was the most rewarding experience of all because of the dedication exhibited by the girls. He coached his last season for the high school in 1995.

Once George left high school coaching, he set out with Peg to re-open the local ski slope in the small Cape Breton town. Despite the fact that the community-owned and community-run Cape Smokey was losing money when it closed down, George said, 'Let's open it, lose less money and create winter jobs in the region.' David Rasmussen noted that George 'invested a lot of himself in the hill, as he did with everything that he took on', but ultimately was unable to make the effort stick. By 1998, the couple sold their investments in Nova Scotia and returned to the United States.

Oneonta and the National Soccer Hall of Fame

AFTER MOVING back to the US in 1998, George and Peggy settled in Oneonta, New York, where the National Soccer Hall of Fame was located at the time. Both George, in his roles on the board of directors and as acting president, and Peg as the archive manager, contributed a great deal to the success of the original National Soccer Hall of Fame. First opened in 1979, the National Soccer Hall of Fame established its first public exhibits in an interim museum on Ford Avenue in Oneonta. In 1983, the US Soccer Football Association officially acknowledged Oneonta's efforts and sanctioned the Hall of Fame.

And 1990 saw the construction of the 61-acre Wright National Soccer Hall of Fame Campus. The ensuing years were packed with fundraising and development efforts. In 1994 the organisation was declared the 'Official Historian' to the USSFA and 'Official Repository' of 1994 World Cup cultural heritage. The Hall of Fame grew from a small storefront museum to an $8m complex constructed in 1999 that included the USSF Hall of Fame, a 30,000-square-foot building. It housed a museum, interactive game area, retail store, library, archives and administrative offices.

By 2000, five major exhibits were added to the facility along with a playing field concession plaza that included food services, a satellite store, office, officials' lounge and bathrooms. Surrounding playing fields, stadium grandstands, dressing rooms and showering facilities came a few years later. The Hall of Fame selection process initially started with the Philadelphia Old Timers' Association in 1950. Between 1950 and 2001, a total of 96 players and 128 builders were inducted.

George created the newsletter, *The Hall of Famer*, and, during his one-year presidency, he oversaw the largest induction in the Hall of Fame's history, which featured Mia Hamm and Julie Foudy. Of particular significance was his development of a major sponsorship with the Century Council's *Girl Talk: Choices and Consequences of Underage Drinking* which underwrote the entire induction. His years on the board of directors were focused on the best ways to promote and fund the Hall of Fame and to differentiate it from the slightly more well-known Baseball Hall of Fame half an hour north in Cooperstown.

In 2002, the National Soccer Hall of Fame teamed up with Pathfinder Village, a 100-year-old community that helps people with Down's syndrome and other disabilities discover their own talent. Pathfinder Village created a soccer team along with the Hall of Fame to host clinics on the Wright Campus for children with disabilities, giving hands-on instruction and coaching advice to help the children develop their interest in soccer. George and Peg enthusiastically agreed to help coach the team as it was a great way for the children to develop confidence, work as a team, and just have fun. Throughout his association with Exxon, no matter where he was moved to, George helped to establish and run youth soccer leagues – whether in Houston with the Inwood Dads Club, Colorado, Libya, Saudi Arabia, or in New Jersey.

The dedication that George and Peggy showed toward the Hall of Fame inspired many at all levels within the sport. This chapter concludes with some of those testimonials from leaders within the US soccer community.

'During my ten-year tenure as secretary-general of US Soccer, I have witnessed the growth of our game and its National Soccer Hall of Fame. While many people may take some credit for the growth of the importance of the Hall, George Brown played a leadership role in establishing the Hall as an important part of the American soccer culture.

'Every year at the Hall of Fame induction ceremony, George and Peg would host our annual Liars' Club Retreat. They would open their home and invite all Hall of Famers to come and tell tall tales about their careers. For many, they become the soul of the Hall. It was terrific fun. While I was never a team-mate of George, I knew of his playing. He had a strong reputation. He played in the ethnocentric leagues of New York and New England. Naturally as his dad was a Hall of Famer, he was well known.

'Once I met George in person, I was very impressed. I found him to be of exceptional character. He was a very intelligent and highly successful businessman. I found this to be a rare combination in our sport. He is a soccer gentleman. I gravitated toward him and hopefully befriended him. The Brown family has a great heritage in the game. Indeed, while many people may take credit for the growth of the game and the Hall, George's strong hand and gentlemanly leadership helped make the Hall what it is today. He was a founder.'

Hank Steinbrecher, former secretary-general of US Soccer (1990–2000) and National Soccer Hall of Famer, class of 2005

'I was initially interested in soccer history (history is a topic in which I generally have an interest) because of the 1950 game where the US men's national team beat England at the Brazil World Cup. I had met Walter Bahr and Harry Keough (1950 USMNT players) at the Coaches' Association convention. In the late 1970s, while teaching at the Hun School of Princeton, I met Al Colone. Through the mid-1980s, when I was teaching and coaching in New Jersey, Virginia, and Maine, I met and talked with Colone at many of the conventions. Once I started teaching at Skidmore College, I would come and help at the Hall of Fame in the mid-to-late 1980s. In May of 2000, I started working at the Hall of Fame at the invitation of Will Lunn. I was inspired by Hank Steinbrecher's opening speech and that's when I first met George and Peggy. We did what we could do to build and make the Hall grow. We felt like crusaders, and the National Soccer Hall of Fame was our crusade.

'There were day-to-day conversations with George about how the Hall could move forward. Our bigger conversations, with soccer historian Roger Allaway, were how can we make an election process that had credibility to build a voting pool that might help us engender that credibility, because they [veteran players] participated and saw that it was open and transparent. We would prepare the Hall of Fame ballot materials and follow up with the veterans. The first year, it was limited to only four candidates and with George we developed a philosophy that the hard part should be getting off the ballot and on to the wall and not to get on the ballot! The more people on the ballot, the higher the recognition for the people that rise to the top and that this would be the best way to move forward.

'The year that George took over as administrator, the year that Julie Foudy and Mia Hamm were elected, we got our first real commercial partner, Century Council Group. George did a great job on the business side, creating a great partnership. Throughout the whole time, it was terrific to work with Peg and figure out what was in the archive. By the end, every box had her hand-written notations about its contents. If we didn't know we had an object, we couldn't properly present history, so she did the Hall of Fame a great service. With museums, you always need to have a new project, a new item with a story to put on display. You need to give people a reason to come back, and that's one of the challenges that I discussed with George – giving people a reason to come back. That meant we needed to find funds to build new exhibits. This was among our greater challenges. George helped me negotiate the challenges in my head of the realities of life and business together.'

Jack Huckel, former director of the National Soccer Hall of Fame

'Peg was one of the nicest, most sincere people I've known. Peg volunteered wherever help was needed, especially in our extensive archive. I think of her and George as a team, him serving as our liaison with the old-guard Hall of Famers and as a board member and Peg as everything else. They were generous donors of their time and money. It amazed me that they pulled up stakes and moved to Oneonta to help create the new National Soccer Hall of Fame and Museum. George was a very hands-on board member, especially involved with the operations staff. He also served on the finance committee and put his corporate experience to work in that role.

'To me one of the most significant contributions George made in preserving the history of the sport predated my involvement. (I was initially hired by the board of directors in 1990 as a full-time consultant to spearhead the effort to raise the funds and build the new museum. I was appointed president in 1996 and served in that capacity until 2006.) George brought his father, James, to Oneonta, in the mid-to-late 1980s I believe, and moderated an interview between Hall of Famers James Brown and Arnie Oliver, the only living members of the 1930 US World Cup team known at that time. I think George told me the two had not seen each other in over 50 years, since their trip to Montevideo, Uruguay. Their meeting and interview was videotaped, and that oral/video history is a priceless artefact of US soccer history.'

Will Lunn, former president/CEO of the National Soccer Hall of Fame

'Visitors were always so surprised and pleased to meet a Hall of Famer, so we would often ask George to come in and speak when we knew we had a bus arriving or an event with youth in the Hall. George always tried to accommodate the request because he knew it was an important way to connect with the public and made the visit special. George would proudly talk about his dad being a Hall of Famer, showing off his kit on display and discussing the memories his dad had passed on to him about those early days on the USSF team. Then George would let people know he was a Hall of Famer too, the time period he played, and the famous people who he played with and against. His stories would bring the black and white photos in the exhibits to life and the listeners were spellbound by his mastery of the tale.

'Peggy was the stalwart archivist that the Hall needed to take thousands of archival items and identify and catalogue them. She volunteered for this position and spent thousands of hours working diligently to achieve order. A process that had been started by many over the years on paper and in rudimentary databases was taken to a professional level by

Peggy. She tirelessly organised the collection, worked with soccer historians who would reach out to the Hall for primary resources, and helped exhibitors find the items needed for updating or creating displays.

'The Browns constituted the very soul of the Hall – they wanted to preserve and to shine a light on the history of the sport in America, and their presence helped do that in immeasurable ways. The Browns would hold gatherings around inductions at their home where the returning Hall of Famers, many of whom were not household names, could meet and talk to the new inductees. These soirées were so meaningful for both the older Hall of Famers and the new inductees who often felt the game started with them, and it gave all a richer perspective.

'George and Peggy made this happen in a way that no one else could have. Being a Hall of Famer himself, he could convince the older generations to come, and the younger players were really happy to spend time in a casual atmosphere surrounded by the living history of the sport just before they would become a part of the Hall of Fame. George and Peggy Brown made the Hall of Fame in Oneonta a very special place to visit, and they were cherished by all who encountered them.'

Kathryn Dailey, former director of operations of the National Soccer Hall of Fame

'I first met George and his wife, Peg, after being inducted at the 2003 ceremony at the original National Soccer Hall of Fame in Oneonta, New York. The Browns hosted a private evening to get together with the veterans and new inductees. You felt so welcome at their home. The Hall of Fame was a great first step towards accumulating the most important items, memories and people (players, administrators or builders like myself, and officials) of US soccer's past.

'It was a fraternity to attend the Liars' Club Retreat evening at George and Peg's home – as long as you could find their house! Once you were in, you were in and whatever was said there, stayed there and no one could call another player or person out on their career. Players were the key elements to the Hall of Fame, driving ticket sales, as well as the hosting of tournaments. I spent a fair amount of time on the voting side, and George as well as the veterans' committee were important input elements to the voting process.

'George had a great sense of humour. Whenever I needed to say things out loud, make sense of something or get a different perspective, George was always there and offered a unique, practical perspective. It was always a joy having George and his wife there, as a part of the process at the Hall of Fame. Meeting the pioneers of American soccer from back in the day was precious. He had a great understanding of the game. The fraternity of inductees was so important and is so special.

'To be able to reach out to current players and interact with past players was tremendously important. We did as much as we could to help preserve and promote the game. We always tried to find the items (like my Cosmos items, for example) that were the most representative of the game and crafted the stories around the items. George and Peg were always so warm and generous and always concerned about the people coming to Oneonta and considered everyone to be their guests – ultimately, always made us feel totally at home. That was so nice to have.'

Ted Howard, Former CONCACAF and NASL administrator and National Soccer Hall of Famer, class of 2003

'My time together with George Brown at the National Soccer Hall of Fame included what I am sure was the high point for him and the march toward what would be the low point. The induction events were intimate events prior to the induction of Mia Hamm. Mia's induction into the Soccer Hall of Fame brought interest from within and outside the United States soccer community.

'Certainly the closing of the Hall of Fame in Oneonta was a disappointment for him. However, the years in Oneonta will prove to be critical to the preservation of the history of soccer in the United States. It provided a safe repository for the countless personal collections that would have been lost without its presence.

'It is in vogue today to talk about "storytelling" but how can stories be told without memory? The American soccer memory is what George and Peg tried to preserve. Soccer in the United States did not start with the NASL or the 1994 World Cup, it is much deeper, more ingrained, and richer to who we are. The gift that George gave us is the proof that soccer has always been an American passion.'

Brendan Moylan, COO of Sports Endeavors, Inc. and former member of the board of directors of the National Soccer Hall of Fame

A Third Generation of Brown Booters

GEORGE AND Peggy Brown had a daughter and two sons. The eldest, Sharon, was born on 19 December 1963 in Greenwich, Connecticut. Sharon was the co-captain of her varsity volleyball team during her senior year at Scotch Plains-Fanwood High School. She was also the first female referee in the Scotch Plains-Fanwood recreational soccer league. She was married to Mike Civile, and they had four children – Michael, Michele, Nathan and Matthew – and one grandchild, Bryce.

The eldest of George and Peggy's two sons, David, was born on 31 March 1965 in Greenwich. As a senior central midfielder, Dave helped lead Scotch Plains-Fanwood High School to the county finals in 1983 and received the school's first annual Johan Neeskens Award. He was also named in the Union County First Team Selection by the Union County Coaches' Association. That year, he was recruited by several colleges, and went on to play at Drew University where he reached the NCAA tournament two years in a row.

Following college, Dave played with numerous teams, including the New Jersey Arrows; Academica in Newark's LISA League – where he helped the team win the second division championship, was named MVP, and played in the league's all-star team; Club Colombia in New Jersey's Latin American League; and the Ridge Rovers team that won the league title in 1993. Following his playing career, Dave went on to referee and coach little league soccer in New Jersey. David is married to Marybeth Joyce and they have three daughters: Emily, Margaret (Maggie) and Cate. Emily and Maggie made varsity in their freshman year of soccer and were named as captains in their senior year.

I am Jim Brown, the youngest of the Brown children. I was born on 30 July 1972 in Greenwich and started playing soccer when I was three years old. I enjoyed avoiding the cold winter games in Houston, Texas, by hiding in the green Volkswagen Westphalia van called Bessy. When George took a position with Exxon in New York in the late 1970s, he decided to settle near Westfield in Scotch Plains, New Jersey. Westfield seems to be the area of many 'starting points' for the development of soccer in this part of the Brown family. Between 1982 and 1984, I played local soccer while living in Saudi Arabia and was selected to tour through Europe during a few months in England, Belgium, the Netherlands and Germany. My dad used to attend games in the Dhahran compound and record my movements during the game with a tape recorder, like a sports commentator.

When I moved back to the US to New Jersey, I was the leading scorer at Terrill Middle School in 1985 and the second-highest scorer in 1986. From there I followed my siblings on to Scotch Plains-Fanwood High School, where I was selected for the varsity soccer team as a freshman in 1987. With Scotch Plains-Fanwood I was part of two state championships and named captain in my senior year – after having switched from striker to sweeper halfway through the four-year high school period. In the first unofficial summer training with the high school team before the start of the freshman year, coach Tom Breznitsky asked if I was Dave's brother. What pressure – and it didn't get any easier.

All the comments about being the brother of David Brown fill my dressing room memories from the start of my freshman year, back during the first week of being selected to the varsity team. There was 'a lot of work to do in order to fill his shoes'. During lunch, I used to sit by myself and read the newspaper. One day 'Brez' Breznitsky came into the lunch room and sat down across from me. My fellow freshman soccer team-mates were only a table or two away, but close enough to hear. He asked how things were going and had one question to ask me, 'Would I like to play varsity soccer?'

Would I ever! Of course, my team-mates across the way heard all of this and treated me as a kiss-up! I said how could I kiss up when he approached me?! What would they have said in my place? They were just envious, I guess. But that meant that I had to play the full freshman and varsity schedules and train between matches and on weekends. That freshman year I played with the likes of Vic Passucci, Joe Mortarulo, and Lino DiCuollo, future All-American at Rutgers University and currently the MLS senior vice-president of competition and player relations. He and Vic introduced everyone on the team to the technique of *Wiel Coerver*, a type of step-over-the-ball footwork to deceive opponents and throw them off balance. We won Scotch Plains-Fanwood's first state championship in 1987, and never looked back.

My style and my play grew stronger with every summer that passed after playing for many years with David and his high school team-mates, who were at least six to seven years older than me. Nothing like getting knocked around in the back yard to force you to adapt and improve your game. The back yard was about the size of a five-a-side pitch. There were times when even Grandpa Brown used to come on the field in the back yard to have one or two kicks of the ball at the house on Cooper Road in Scotch Plains, trailing a bottle of oxygen alongside since he had developed emphysema from smoking unfiltered cigarettes since a teen in NYC. As one team-mate, Jason Hills, said of our house in Scotch Plains at the time:

'Going to the Browns' house when growing up in Scotch Plains, New Jersey, was like walking into a soccer oasis. It wasn't just that soccer was spoken of often … it wasn't just those little TVs that pocketed the house, constantly playing Premier League games even when no one was sitting in the room on the off chance that someone walking by could catch another kick … it was that the entire family ate, slept and breathed the beautiful game. It had become a way of life for them. For all of them. If something fell in the back yard neither Dave nor James reached down to pick it up but would rather flick it up with one of their feet tricks.

'"Barefoot soccer" became our favourite summer pastime for hours on end, for days in a row. Perhaps my favourite memories of all are when George would come out and play with us, but of course we would never call him that. It was always "Mr Brown". Even well into his 50s, he would school us on the pitch. I remember once when he was guarding me, feeling him kicking slightly at my legs and tugging on my shorts. I said, "Mr Brown! What are you doing?" He smiled in the way only he could and said, "This is how the game is played on the highest levels. You'd better get used to it." Then I remember visiting Jim's family in Oneonta and playing soccer golf in his back yard, because even into his 70s, Mr Brown loved the game with all of his heart. He smiled and reminded us of how his father would "play goal post" because he was too old to play any other position! Now, I am the one playing goal post!

'I learned in these sacred days that soccer can be a way of life. Soccer can be the glue that knits boys to their fathers and friends to other friends. I did not just learn how to play the game, I learned how to live it, and this is a legacy I have passed down to my friends and colleagues over the past three decades. I owe my ability and vision to do this to the Brown household.'

My father George was a constant back yard player in the mid-1980s and his clever shielding of the ball and eventual 'flooring' of opponents – 'accidental' of course – was legendary.

Since my freshman year, I was primarily a forward. My height and speed helped to score goals here and there. In the summer of my junior year, when I was 17, I attended a two-week soccer camp in Connecticut for the second year in a row along with a few of my high school team-mates. About a week into the camp something clicked, and I decided that I had had enough of getting my legs swiped out from under me as a forward and I switched to defence. Well, when we started summer camp for the upcoming high school season, my team-mates who were at the camp with me told Brez he should think about putting me in the defence and that was that.

I was locked into the starting XI in a team that I had personally played with for the past six years every spring in club matches and knew them well. I learned a lot from sweeper Todd Kylish, and midfielders Larry Naldi and Rick Emery in my new defensive role. We won our second state championship in 1989 with an all-senior starting line-up, except for me, in my junior year. We beat our rivals Westfield at home 3-2, and it was a flawless season aside from a single 1-0 loss to an unstoppable St Benedict's team that was powered by future US men's national team captain Claudio

Reyna. This team was by far the most influential for me, throughout my four-year career. They were smart, creative, pretty cool and knew the game of soccer.

The off-season and summer months were spent playing with a great group of friends: Jason Hills, Paul Pace, Brackie Reyes, Jose Sanchez-Mariscal, Erik Klein Robertello, Corey Brelinski, Keith Joy and Shimme Wexler. Everywhere we could get a pick-up game, we'd be up for it – Tamaques Park during torrential downpours, or AT&T Bell Laboratories with co-workers of Bill Ochs (a former SPFHS team-mate of David), in an over-20 league.

In my senior year, the season started off well. We beat Westfield 2-1 on their home turf, and TV 3 commentator Hugh Albanesius mentioned in the player focus before the game stated, '[Brown] has given leadership to the club and held them together and they've been very successful because of it. He's the sweeper, co-captain, has very good speed and also plays on the New Jersey All Select Under-18 Olympic Development Program.' I was so proud to have my grandpa Jimmy in attendance along with my brother, grandma Brown and aunt Marilyn. Dad was normally in attendance. He preferred sitting in the higher section of the bleachers so that he wouldn't have to hear the whining and complaining of all the parents. But no matter where he was sitting, I'd always hear the words of encouragement. I tallied seven goals and five assists during my senior year, as I'd make runs from the back from time to time or go up for corners. Unfortunately, I suffered a ruptured spleen during a match and was out for the remainder of the senior season.

Over a 45-year career, Tom Breznitsky was the second-most successful boys' varsity soccer coach in NJ state history and third-greatest of all time nationally, recording 761 victories. He passed away in 2021. He helped guide Scotch

Plains to seven state titles, 19 sectional championships and 19 Union County Tournament crowns with a 761-185-63 record.

Brez worked tirelessly to help players reach their maximum potential. He was tough, but you were better off for it. Even when you went to college, Brez would often turn up to watch a game here or there with a current Scotch Plains player. Scotch Plains legend Alex Passucci succeeded Brez in 2020.

I managed to come back to play for the mighty Union Lancers two months later in the early winter months of 1991, under Carl Schellscheidt, the son of famous Seton Hall coach and former US national team coach Manfred 'Manny' Schellscheidt. I was selected for the All-County, All-Conference and All-State teams. One reporter from the *Courier* remarked that '[Brown] is everybody's all everything'.

One neat memory was that before and after each title that was won, whether it was the Union County, Sectional or State Championship, our cheerleaders used to come to the house of each player and 'decorate' the front lawn with toilet paper in the trees and signs of encouragement. Of course, they always asked permission from our parents beforehand! I was selected to the New Jersey state team, winning the New Jersey State Gold Cup after marking and beating Claudio Reyna and his team, Elizabeth, and competed in trials for the national development team and national cup competitions. I won a soccer scholarship to attend Rider University and was selected as Rookie of the Year in my freshman year and was guided with the help of Rider's assistant coach, Duane Robinson, also a former Union Lancer and winner of the McGuire Cup in the 1980s.

After college, I played most of the mid-1990s with the German American Kickers in Yardville, Pennsylvania, with my college room-mate and best friend (and brother) to this day, Tarik Hajji. Tarik was quite a technical player and was able to play a lot of one-two give-and-goes with great vision and through balls that left you open-jawed. At GAK, we had fond memories of great games and even greater after-game dinners with the best steaks and toppings you could imagine and a few pints to wash those meals down. Dinners took place in the dance hall/bar situated next to the field.

I also spent time with the Newark Portuguese alongside my brother David. He was the sweeper, and I was the stopper – what a great one-two punch! We also played together at Farcher's Grove in Union, New Jersey, where the only bits of grass were in the corner spots in the four corners of the field. We spent a lot of time kicking large rocks off to the side, but after a hard-fought match great times were always to be had in the clubhouse. Our father George also played at Farcher's Grove and won a championship there in the 1950s, so it's quite interesting that father and sons all played on the same grounds within a 40-year period.

In early 2002, after moving to France, I played for a few years early on in La Ferté-sous-Jouarre and won a league championship, scoring seven goals – mostly from headers. Years later on, I especially enjoyed playing with the town youth by organising pick-up matches and small tournaments along with my best friend in France, Laurent Roriz, a talented attacker who constantly threatens defences. I was married and have a son, Aidan-Emerson, who is almost 15 years old.

A New Generation Takes Up a New Code

THE POPULAR beliefs, although deemed a hoax surrounded by a small truth, are that the origins of rugby involve a schoolboy named William Webb Ellis and the idea that in 1823 at Rugby School, in Rugby, England, Ellis disobeyed the football rules (which allowed the handling of the ball only) when he literally picked up the ball and ran with it, and the codification of rugby football came about in the late 1800s as rules and a proper structure were established. The Ellis myth has never truly been verified but is accepted as an inspiration for the formalisation of rugby as a distinct sport among the football codes in the late 1880s.

While John Bell 'Jock' Brown was a standout goalkeeper over the course of more than a decade before and after World War Two, his two sons forged a different path. Peter 'PC' Currie Brown, born on 16 December 1941 in Troon, and his younger brother, Gordon Brown, born on 1 November 1947 in Irvine Central Hospital – went on to forge their own legacies in the rugby code.

Peter was a rugby captain and a legend on his own merit. He led Scotland to their only back-to-back international wins over England over an eight-day period in 1971, representing Scotland from 1964 to 1973. The *Glasgow Herald* has ranked

Peter as the 20th-greatest rugby player of all time. At club level he played for Gala and West of Scotland.

Ian 'Mighty Mouse' McLauchlan, a former international who represented Scotland at loosehead prop from 1969 to 1979, noted that Peter, 'Always turned out every Saturday because he loved playing club ball. People who saw Peter play seven-a-side rugby were able to see how well-rounded of a player he was. Tremendous hands, running, tackling and his eccentric kicking style that always made it over the ball. On the bus, Peter would often take out a pair of socks, roll them up into a ball and start juggling. On game night, Peter would head to bed early. As a captain, Peter had a different view of the game. He was straightforward – encouraging you to do your best.'

Peter even played football, lining up at centre-forward, with Rugby Rovers against the full Queen's Park 11 at Hampden under the floodlights. He was called up to the national rugby team, leading them as captain and winning the Calcutta Cup for the third time in a row after he successfully kicked a devilishly tight-angled conversion in the last minute. Gordon was on the field at the time and rushed up in an attempt to give Peter a celebration bear hug but was ushered away by Peter – who was intent on keeping his concentration for the final play of the game. That's brotherly love for you! No other forward has scored more points (67) than Peter on the Scottish side, and he is the only captain to have beaten England three times.

Peter's height, handling of the ball and leaping ability set him apart. He often dominated line-outs and was deft at converting penalties.[8] John Gray, the former South of Scotland and Gala player and coach, said of Peter, 'When

8 Footage from this match can be viewed at https://www.youtube.com/watch?v=QKPf8p1Wjl8

in his suit of clothing he looked big, but in a rugby strip he looked much bigger. He had a presence, his handling, passing, tackling, and kicking ability was amazing.' His honours include 27 caps for Scotland (including ten as captain), four Calcutta Cups, and playing on two separate Scotland teams that finished as joint champions in the Five Nations. As a number eight or lock forward he was a proficient, powerful kicker, booting six conversions and 15 penalties during his Scotland career.

Peter missed out on selection for the 1971 British & Irish Lions tour of New Zealand, though he continued to play internationally for two more years for Scotland.

After retiring from rugby, he worked with the Scottish Building Society as chairman, and as a senior chartered accountancy partner at the firm Hogg Thorburn. He served as a citing commissioner for the Six Nations and European Cup. McLauchlan argued, 'Peter contributed so much more to rugby once his career was finished. Peter's influence on rugby as an official for his club, helping, coaching, and running the treasury and as secretary of Gala, which were enormous jobs, was outstanding.' Peter also went on the after-dinner speaking circuit and is still filling up rooms with laughter. He is an avid golfer, following in his dad's footsteps, and enjoys taking portrait photographs and has quite an eye for it. He and his wife, Jill, have three children, Julie, Kerry Lynne Brown, Ross Nichol Currie Brown, and two grandchildren.

A Rise and Fall on the International Stage

GORDON BROWN was as gifted and passionate a rugby player as his older brother Peter, and he is universally considered to be one of the best lock forwards to have played for the British & Irish Lions. He represented the Lions during their worldwide campaigns between 1969 and 1977. The *Glasgow Herald* ranked Gordon, known as 'The Lock', the second-greatest Scottish player of all time out of 50 greats. He was capped 30 times for Scotland between 1969 and 1976 and toured three times with the Lions. He was part of the squad that beat the New Zealand All Blacks in 1971, and also helped take down South Africa on the 1974 tour, scoring eight tries – an unusual feat in any era.

Gordon played rugby on Saturday mornings for his school, Marr College, and football in the afternoons for Ayr Albion. On leaving school at 16 to join the Bank of Scotland as a trainee teller he had to decide which sport to play. By that time, despite featuring as a regular goalkeeper for Troon Waverley and later Troon Juniors, rugby won out and he joined Marr FPs where he quickly became established in the first XV. In 1968 he joined Peter's first club, West of Scotland. Peter moved on that year to pursue his chartered accountancy career in Galashiels, so the brothers never played together until Gordon was capped for Scotland. Back in the day, at 17st (238lb) and 6ft 5in, he was a gifted and intelligent ball-catcher in the middle of the line-out and a renowned scrummager. A unique experience, both within the family and in international competition, came when Gordon replaced Peter in an international against Wales in Cardiff in 1970.

In December 1976 during an inter-district game at Murrayfield, Gordon found himself at the bottom of a pile. With his arms blocked under the bodies, out of nowhere came a knee crashing into his face, bursting it open from nose to hairline. Then followed a boot, metal studs and all, as it stomped into his face. Gordon rose to his feet and, half blinded, went after his assailant, Allan Hardie. Gordon caught Hardie and threw him to the ground. Swinging his right leg, Gordon dealt a glancing blow with his shin. The game was televised, and Gordon was hit with a one-year suspension and never played for Scotland again.

With the suspension, it looked like Gordon would miss the 1977 Lions tour. Gordon was traumatised for decades by that incident and, as his son Rory recounted, he was only able to come to terms with that lingering demon while participating in a meditation session during a weekend retreat with his wife Linda. Gordon was banned from training with his club for three months. During that period he battled a hamstring injury. That's when Jock Wallace of Glasgow Rangers FC jumped in to help Gordon.

Wallace had Gordon run up and down the Ibrox Stadium steps, until Gordon begged to stop – and definitely after Gordon had violently thrown up numerous times. Finally, at the end of the gruelling sessions, Gordon felt as light as a feather, seeming to be stronger and faster. Gordon made the 1977 Lions team that summer, but New

Zealand ended their 1970s domination with a 3-1 defeat in the Test series.

Many intriguing stories came out of Gordon's rugby career and especially from his time on the 1971 and 1974 tours. The most famous, certainly, was the Lions' famous battle cry '99' (an abbreviation of the 999 emergency call number back home), which is weaved into rugby folklore, as a retaliation for decades of pushing opponents' physical and mental limits by South Africans. The principle is this: get your retaliation in first, so when a team-mate was in trouble, '99' was called and it worked. If the first line went in for a tussle with the opponent, then the whole team joined in. That way the referee would have had to discipline the whole team, rather than just one or two players. It didn't happen often, because opponents knew what they were in for when it was called out.

Halfway through one fierce match against South Africa during the 1974 tour, Gordon pummelled his opposite number, Orange Free State player Johan de Bruyn, with a crushing tackle. With the hit, de Bruyn's glass eye popped out and couldn't be found. Everyone, including the referee, went on their hands and knees to search for the eye. All of the sudden someone cried out, 'Eureka!' Johan grabbed the glass eye, stuck it back in the gaping hole in his face – grass sticking out of the sides and all – and kept on playing.

After one match earlier in his career, on 12 October 1970, Gordon suffered pain in his left shin. The pain persisted and he eventually went for an X-ray. Alistair Wilson, another rugby player, had been complaining of pain as well. The most bizarre thing was found in the X-ray of Gordon's lower leg – Alistair's tooth, root, and all! The two men had played against one another the week before. Gordon said he would keep the tooth in his pocket and return it the next time he saw Alistair.

Like most of the Brown clan, Gordon was a proficient golfer and boasted a low handicap. He even played with the legendary Gary Player while in South Africa in the 1970s. After his rugby career ended, he became a prominent after-dinner speaker and, as usual, the life of the party. One such after-dinner speech came at the request of Manchester United in the late 1990s. With the evening in full swing, Gordon turned to United's chairman at the time, Martin Edwards, and said, 'You know, Martin, my uncle, Jimmy Brown, played under Scott Duncan in the early 1930s.' Then he proceeded to tell the story about Duncan boarding the cruise liner and stealing Jimmy away from the Partick Thistle manager. Edwards was so enthralled by the story that he rushed out of the room and disappeared for a while. He had ducked out to the archives area to verify this amazing story; sure enough, it was all true.

Gordon's height and weight easily made him stand out in a crowd, not to mention his infectious smile and hardy laugh. His laughter and non-stop storytelling was contagious and loved by many. Gordon worked as part of the ITV World Cup commentary teams in 1991 and 1995. He wrote a book filled with the great stories and anecdotes that accompanied him throughout his illustrious career.

Gordon was diagnosed with non-Hodgkin's lymphoma and passed away at 53 on 19 March 2001 in the Ayr hospice for which he had raised funds during his life. His funeral was held in Troon, and he was so beloved in the community that the church was bursting at the seams. Hundreds more were forced to gather outside, and those in attendance included family, celebrities, rugby team-mates and even past opponents to celebrate Gordon's life.

At a wonderful dinner held three weeks before he died, in front of 1,400 people in the Great Room at London's Grosvenor Hotel, Johan de Bruyn presented Gordon with the glass eye from their 1974 match mounted on a specially made trophy. A memorial garden and sitting area in a local Troon park was dedicated by the then prime minister Tony Blair's wife, Cherie Blair. He is survived by his wife Linda, their two children, Mardi and Rory, and the apple of his eye, grandson Zac. Gordon was inducted into the Scottish Rugby Hall of Fame, the International Rugby Hall of Fame, and the World Rugby Hall of Fame.

Let's close the chapter with the words of Rory, who is also the curator of the Gordon Brown Rugby Collection, who summed up his father's legacy and the family's broader success in sports in his own inimitable way:

'I've always found it a difficult question to answer, what's it like having Gordon Brown for a dad? My immediate thought was always I don't know. He's ma dad. I don't have another dad to compare him to. Now in my 44th year and having lost ma dad 22 years ago I am now starting to see him from everyone else's point of view. His achievements in sport were "normal" in the "Broons' Hoose". Uncle Peter captained Scotland at rugby and Grampie "Jock" Brown was a professional footballer. Sporting ability runs through my mother's side as well. Her father, Willie Hastings, was a professional golfer (who turned down signing for Rangers) and ma aunt Joan captained the British ladies' golf team. Both ma grandpas played in the same school football team that won the Scottish schools trophy.

'Even just watching sport was a learning experience in itself, listening to my family commentate as to how it "should" be done. "Stick in 'til ye stick out. Get stuck in but play to the rules. Don't cheat." Good life advice. Grampa was one of the first goalkeepers in football to come off his line to narrow the angle (I have heard he was the first). "Six foot two, eyes of blue, big Jock Broon is comin fur you!"

'Growing up in Troon was great. Playing on the beach all year round. Kicking balls barefoot on the sand and diving off the rocks by the harbour until we turned blue. We had freedom to roam and wherever we went a gran or grampa's house was never far away for a bite to eat or something fizzy to drink. These were the same streets all ma grandparents played on which also made it a difficult place for me to hide. I remember visiting Grampie Brown as he was heading out for a walk one stormy day. He was 90 years old and was always a believer in "you've got to keep your legs moving". He was blind in one eye and even his good eye was nae that good. Will you be OK Grampa? Will I come with you? "Son," he says. "I've been walking these streets ma whole life. Thanks, but I'll be fine." Later on, I saw him walking along the beachfront with his bunnet and shoulder dipped into the wind and rain coming off the sea. I would always stop if I saw Grampie but this time I just watched him in his natural habitat and absorbed the moment, ingraining the image in my memory.

'As a child the Broons and their mother would beach comb after a storm. There was usually some bounty washed up. In particular sea coal. Ayrshire is rich in coal and there is a natural seam of the black stuff off the west coast which would often wash up in wee chunks after a storm. It would be bagged up and taken home. This is the same beach where we would play "sodgies" (soldiers). The same beach Grampa patrolled at night when the Germans were threatening to invade. His mother was a midwife and was usually disturbed in the middle of the night to attend a local in labour. Young

Jock would be woken to escort his mother in the dark. Especially when she was required to go up by the harbour as it was dangerous then. Ships from all over the world would be docked there. China, Russia and South America to name a few. Ma grampa would often hear sailors' requests of how much for the boy? And the fear of being sold was real as they had nothing. A successful baby delivery didn't always mean getting paid either. Shoes were only used in winter. Dinner cooked over an open fire. How my childhood differed. I always thought he was raised in medieval times.

'He always had time for a kick-about in his garden. A game of three and down the green. Goalposts made out of driftwood and old fishing nets and loads of repaired footballs. All found at the beach. The war really put a stop to his blossoming football career as he joined the navy just after winning the Scottish Cup with Clyde. In his final years he expressed how much it hurt. War really got in the way of life and his playing career. We were pals. We played golf together where the winner would buy lunch. It would usually end in a half. The winner to be decided next time. As a physio he worked at Kilmarnock FC where Peter, John and Gordon would help paint the terracing in the summer holidays. He remained true to his beginnings in life though and me and him would always be in the Ayr end for an Ayrshire derby. Mon Ayr! Away ye go referee! He would shout with a wee wink.

'Then once a year to the Ayr races for a wee punt on the horses and a bag o' chips on the way home. He was a positive man with a strength and a gentleness about him that was obvious in ma dad as well. I remember having a great night out in Paris with ma dad when I was 16 when the mood quickly changed. We were confronted by a large rowdy group late at night after an international match. "If anything happens wee man, you run and I'll take out the first five." He was serious but was totally calm and there was no doubt that the first five were getting it! We weren't raised to start trouble.

'In the house in Troon when I was wee, he would hardly be through the front door when I would be harassing him for a kick-about. Even if it was dark outside the hallway would do. As I grew the hallway got smaller. Eventually the hallway wasn't big enough for the two of us. "Move!" "Naw, you move!" Battle ensues. Maw Broon steps in and kicks us both out the back door where some quick rules of war were established (no punching in the face) and on with the show. It wasn't violence, it was how we bonded. We never ever fell out with each other. I had the pleasure of travelling with him when he was going all over the world doing his after-dinner speaking.

'This is when our friendship was truly sealed, and people would often comment on how nice it was to see us getting on so well. We did. We laughed a lot. Just two boys on tour having fun. Everywhere he went I would hear, "Awright big man!" "There's Broonie!" And he would speak back as if he knew them all. "Who's that, Dad?" "I dunno," would be the reply. People would gravitate towards him where they would be welcomed with warmth and humour. Laughter was everything. He would also make a great wind break. Whenever he came to watch me play football or rugby there was usually a dozen other parents standing downwind of him sheltering from the weather. When I played games in rougher parts of Ayrshire, getting out alive wasn't always a given. The whole team would breathe a sigh of relief when he appeared on the touchline. Gordon's here, we'll be fine! He would just laugh and say it was exactly the same when he was young.

'Now I'm a bit older and a father myself I am starting to look back on how incredible ma dad's life was. If he saw you in the street and you needed help, he would be the first to assist. When he died, we were sent amazing messages from so many people recounting stories of when he helped them in their time of need. Stories we were oblivious to. His sporting achievements have also stood the test of time. He was great but he is also considered the greatest. And after all these years I can finally answer the question. It was absolutely magic having Gordon Brown as ma dad.'

The Lambie Connection

ISABELLA BELL, James's mother, had a sister named Mary Don Carmichael Bell (born in 1900 and passed away in 1975) who married Alex 'Alec' Lambie on 27 April 1923 in Troon. Alex (born 15 April 1897 in Troon) was a passionate and well-admired, 'solid and dependable' centre-half and captain for Partick Thistle from 1921 to 1931. He served in the Royal Scots Fusiliers during World War One in Gallipoli and the Dardanelles with the Gurkha Regiment. In 1920 he played briefly with Kilmarnock, and was part of the squad that won the Scottish Cup. With First Division Partick Thistle he made 330 appearances, scoring 20 goals and won the Glasgow Charity Cup in 1927; was capped for a Scottish League XI against an English League XI in 1928; and in the same year, he took part in the last Home Scots v Anglo-Scots international trial match, but this was not considered a full cap, and he went to the Scottish Cup Final in April 1930. Again during the 1934/35 season, he won the Glasgow Charity Cup. He played with Dreghorn, Kilmarnock, Troon Athletic, Partick Thistle, Chester, Swindon Town, Lovell's Athletic and Distillery throughout his career until 1934.

Alex 'Sanny' Lambie was also pretty well-known in Ayr, where he owned a very popular chip shop around the corner from Ayr United's Somerset Park. 'Sanny' comes from the Christian name of Alexander, like Zander in Scotland. He was fondly remembered by his cousins, Peter and John Brown, as he sat perched on his chair in the chip shop, called the Seagull Cafe, in the morning, endlessly peeling potatoes and cutting chips, located on Content Street. He had a wooden leg as a result of an injury during his Partick Thistle days. It went septic and eventually required an amputation in order for Sanny to survive. He passed away in 1965 in Troon.

Alex was known as a player who was powerful in the air and on the ground. Standing six feet tall and weighing 16st (224lb), he was never the quickest player on the pitch but his enthusiasm helped in making tackles just when opponents thought they had beaten him. As the *Daily Record* described, 'Lambie is a man and a half. He seems to spread himself all over the field. He lashes out at everything, and very much more often than not gets what he goes out for.' As early as 1921, Alex was mentioned as being one of the best as he played outside-left and was 'a worry' for the opposition in Stevenston United's match against Johnstone.

Alex netted for Stevenston in a 2-1 loss on Valentine's Day 1921 against East Fife. Partick Thistle signed Lambie, who was noted as a player who should 'blossom into a centre half-back of the highest grade'. He also played a few trials for Ayr United and took Kilmarnock's 'shilling' before returning to Troon Athletic. Dundee's match against Partick saw Lambie appear for Thistle again. He saw one 'great drive' blocked, and later pounced on a weak header by Jackson only for Aimer to come to Dundee's rescue and clear.

Thistle started off the 1923/24 season with a historic 2-1 win against Celtic, having never previously beaten the Glasgow club in a league encounter. The comparatively small Celtic forwards were disadvantaged as the tall trio of Chatton, Lambie and Gibson got everything in the air with the Celts not keeping the ball low enough. Lambie distinguished himself from the other two forwards by keeping the ball more on the floor.

Raith Rovers' Jennings was no match for Lambie on 21 January 1924. He was very clever in the first half, but later on was dominated by the 6ft centre-half, who had an outstanding game. Two months later Partick Thistle drew 1-1 with Hibernian in front of a crowd of 30,000. The match lasted for two hours. Hibs scored early in the first half and the Jags fought to equalise. Nine minutes from time, Lambie – standing out from a mob of players excitedly scrambling in front of Hibs' goal – lifted the ball over their heads into the net. On 17 April Lambie nodded in a header right before half-time against Hibernian in the Scottish Cup. Alex played in a footballers' golf tournament on 15 May. He was beaten by one hole in the first round by Kyle.

Partick kicked off the 1924/25 season against Hibernian on 24 August, losing 3-2. Lambie took a shot from 30 yards, which Harper did well to pick from underneath the crossbar. A month later, Thistle drew against Rangers in the Glasgow Cup semi-final in front of 30,000 fans. Lambie towered over his opponents, Henderson and Cairns, proving to be a real menace to their success. In the replay the following day, the Jags fell 1-0. Lambie was heavily involved, taking a shot towards goal in the first minute, but Robb made a great save. On 21 December Lambie helped Thistle force the game against Falkirk from the half-back position. He had more shots on goal in the first half than any other player, and his heading was brilliant. The heavy ground suited Lambie.

His 1926 started out particularly well. Thistle sent Motherwell out of the Scottish Cup and Lambie was the best of the 22 players on 24 January, according to the *Sunday Post*. He scored two goals, and the writer of the article said that he was the star and a revelation to him. He had known Lambie's worth as a defensive centre-half, and that day he was with an equal, both as an attacker and defender. The writer had a lot to say for the failure of Motherwell's forwards. Lambie was the driving force in the half-back line. His defensive tactics and his urging of his forwards were equally effective against St Mirren on 21 February.

Thistle beat Rangers 6-3 to win the Glasgow Merchants Charity Cup in front of 18,599 spectators on 15 May. Alec Hair scored five of the six goals and Lambie was the most outstanding man apart from Hair, but the whole team rose to the occasion. In the ninth minute, Lambie broke out to the right from his centre-half position and steadied for a nice pass in the middle for Hair to put away. Rangers could make no headway against Lambie and his defence. A week later, Lambie was re-signed after being placed on Thistle's transfer list despite his performances.

In the 28 February 1928 Scottish Cup quarter-final, Thistle had faced Queen's Park. The *Sunday Post* supplement for the match mentioned that Lambie was the outstanding personality of his squad. Tall and whole-hearted, 'Alec' could 'worry any centre-forward'. Lambie captained Partick Thistle 'with fine judgement' against a strong Queen's Park side as they fell 1-0 at Hampden Park on 3 March.

On 12 March, Lambie lined up for Scotland against England at Ibrox. He policed England's Dixie Dean for three-quarters of the match but found the pace to be too much. England's forwards took advantage of Lambie sticking to Dean 'like a brother' and knocked in a few goals, winning 6-2. All of the goals were scored in the second half. The Scots were incapable of holding their own, and England's speed forced their opponents off balance. One main problem was that they were without their 'Anglos' – the Scots who were not released from their English clubs for the match.

Thistle beat Motherwell 2-0 on 6 April to harm their chances of winning the championship. The Jags had Lambie to thank, as Motherwell's men had no time to think things through. As *The Motherwell* noted, 'Lambie's opening was very moderate, but what an ending! The big Queen's Cross man finished up the best half on view … his lusty punting turned defence into attack.'

Saturday, 19 May found Alex enjoying his second passion, golf, at the footballers' golf tournament at Troon. It was one of the most exciting tournaments in recent memory. J. M'Ilwane, of Portsmouth, who was competing in his first tournament, defeated Alex, who had been familiar with the Troon course since childhood. Lambie displayed a superior short game, and was three up at the turn, and one up at the 17th hole. Lambie found the bunker, and M'Ilwane took advantage. On that same green Lambie had great chances to win the match but was two yards short with his approach putt and failed to get down with his next attempt, meaning the match was squared. Over 100 onlookers followed the action as they made their way to the final hole. M'Ilwane drove well down the fairway, and Lambie topped his first and second shots. M'Ilwane won the hole easily in five shots.

An interesting note is that the consolation handicap winners included Alex James, the then Preston North End forward who within the next decade became Arsenal's saving grace, helping them to win two FA Cups, and turning himself into an everlasting football legend. He was known for the excellent quality of his passing and supreme ball control. The young James Brown, if you remember, was once compared to Alex James at the beginning of his career with Manchester United in 1932.

On 22 October Partick Thistle played some convincing football and knocked more than the ball around in the

2-0 win against Clyde. There was never a dull moment as Thistle opened with a rush and scored within the first minute. Clyde kept on fighting, but Partick's defence held them back. Some 10,000 spectators saw Alex Lambie collect a free kick that landed in the penalty box, which he rightly headed into the net to seal Clyde's fate. Towards the end of the year, Thistle dominated and Lambie captained his squad throughout the Glasgow Dental Cup, beating Third Lanark 1-0 on 6 November before a crowd of 1,000 spectators; on 28 November they beat Celtic 3-1 at Hampden Park, before 3,000; finally, Partick beat Rangers 2-0 in front of 8,000 to win the cup on 11 December.

The 26 January 2-0 loss at Cowdenbeath saw the Jags struggle on hard winter ground in front of a crowd of 2,000. Cowdenbeath were more aggressive and took more risks. Lambie provided great midfield work, but Partick's forwards couldn't break through Cowdenbeath's defensive line. At this point, Partick were in tenth place with 23 points after ten wins and nine losses.

February saw the Jags win two, lose one and draw one. By mid-March, Partick were in sixth place with 30 points and accumulating 14 wins, 11 losses and five draws. From January to mid-March, forwards Johnny Ballantyne (five goals), John Torbet (six) and Harry Gibson (five) were in good form. Ballantyne had left Thistle in 1924 to play with the Boston Soccer Club until 1928, when US professional soccer was gaining success with a large club expansion on the East Coast and US teams poaching talent from Great Britain, notably Scotland. He returned to the Jags in 1929 until 1935.

Partick would end March with a 5-0 defeat to Aberdeen and then they started April with two more losses. In the Scottish Cup Partick didn't get past the second round but they met Rangers in the final of the Glasgow Charity Cup at Ibrox Park, in front of a crowd of 12,000. Gate receipts for charitable causes were £2,670. The day hampered both sides with high winds and heavy rain, but Rangers struck first within the first minute as they had the wind at their backs. Thistle made a 'spirited' rally, but their defence couldn't hold their opponents as Rangers were awarded a penalty and never looked back. In the dying minutes, however, Ballantyne scored to at least get Thistle a goal. Thistle would end the 1928/29 league season in sixth place with 38 points.

The 1929/30 season started out well in August with Partick winning two matches, scoring a combined eight goals, losing one and drawing one. Their 21 September game against Heart of Midlothian, in front of a crowd of 20,000, ended in a 2-1 win, in which Barney Battles Jr, formerly a team-mate of Ballantyne at Boston, scored for Hearts. By this stage of the season, striker John Simpson had scored ten times for Thistle.

On 22 September, Thistle were beaten for only the second time all season, losing 2-1 to Aberdeen. By mid-October, Thistle sat in sixth place with ten points. In the *Weekly News* edition of 9 November, the writer, who called himself 'Number One', spoke about the Partick 'stalwarts' and Lambie tipping the scale as the heftiest of them all at 6ft 2in and 14st. He had arguably been one of Scotland's leading midfielders for many seasons, and his use of his head and effective tackling was consistent proof that he was a formidable obstacle for any attacking centre-forward. On 16 November Partick lost 4-1 to Queen's Park, but Lambie was 'the outstanding man' on the visitors' side. The 1 December match between Thistle and St Johnstone ended in a 1-1 draw, but Lambie was effective in halting the dangerous runs of the Saints strikers. Lambie's height was a huge asset during aerial duels in the midfield and defensive ends.

December seemed to be Lambie's month as he contained the opposition, one after the other, particularly when Partick beat St Mirren 3-0 on 14 December. St Mirren gave it all they had, often with reckless abandon, yet Thistle's defence held the line, with Lambie as the 'bulkhead'. Christmas Day pitted Thistle against Queen's Park, with the Jags stealing a 1-0 victory at Firhill Park in front of a crowd of 18,000. Partick ended the year in fourth.

The first round of the Scottish Cup got under way for Partick with a 6-1 thrashing of Dalbeattie Star on 18 January before a paying crowd of 2,100. The pitch was troublesome in spots and didn't allow Thistle to demonstrate their true potential, but they scored their first goal after three minutes and dominated, so much so that their goalkeeper Johnny Jackson didn't even touch the ball for the first 30 minutes.

In the second round, Thistle took on formidable Dundee United and won 3-0 before 8,573 at Tannadice Park. High hopes gave way to despair early on for United fans as it was clear that their team were not on the Jags' level. Teamwork and craft enabled Thistle to navigate through muddy waters, literally, and had the surface been firmer then the score could have been greater. Lambie was strong in the midfield as the 'sheet-anchor of the line'. Thistle's Scottish Cup matches in January and February saw forwards John Torbet and David Ness score three and four goals each to lead the Jags.

Alex was then out sick for a period, but he was back in full force against Aberdeen in the 15 February Scottish Cup match that saw Partick beat Aberdeen 3-2. 'Lady Luck' seemed to be on their side from the start to the final whistle. Tensions were high and Aberdeen were the better team, but captain Lambie dominated in the air and ran rings around the opposition. He even got off a few shots. The crowd of 39,568 fans gripped their seats and held their breath for 90 minutes. In the semi-final Thistle battled Hamilton Academical at Celtic Park, winning 3-1 in front of a crowd of 37,590 with gate receipts totalling £1,538. The odds were against Partick but they won in a convincing, methodical style. Alex policed the midfield and fed the forward line with Ness showing fine, dangerous form and always being a threat. The Jags always got a head or foot in on Hamilton's attacking efforts. League results were not good in March as Thistle came away with three draws (0-0 with both Hibernian and Falkirk, and 1-1 with Dundee United) and a 4-0 defeat to Motherwell. They seemed to have been concentrating more on the Scottish Cup.

Thistle would then face Rangers at Hampden Park on 12 April in the final of the Scottish Cup. The match-up in front of 107,475 fans was a great duel, back and forth for the full 90 minutes; neither side deserved to lose, and neither did as at the end the score was 0-0.

The crowd got their money's worth with thrilling attacking and midfield battles. One element that disrupted the normal pace was the constant strong breeze ripping up and down the field, slashing from side to side. Thistle were the more stable and harmonious of the two teams with their half-backs and the forward line in sync. Rangers were moreeffective in the first half with numerous chances, but the Jags held tight.

Thistle did a better job in the second half at building up through midfield, with Lambie feeding the ball out to the wide forwards, who streaked down the sidelines and sent in crosses that sliced through the defence. A fingertip save here and the woodwork there – Partick couldn't get the goal they deserved.

The replay would take place on the following Wednesday. A crowd of 102,479 packed Hampden, the highest attendance for any midweek match in Britain. In a twist of fate, Rangers turned the tables on Partick by vastly improving while Thistle did not. They seemed hesitant and not as mobile. Overall, the match was not nearly as exciting as the first meeting, but Rangers proved they were up to the task, even against the wind in the first half. Just before half-time, Rangers broke through Lambie and his crew with a low drive that beat goalkeeper Jackson after having weaved its way through a sea of players and smacked the back of the net. In the second half, John Torbet took an excellent cross from a raid on the right flank and buried the equalising goal. Eighteen minutes from the end, Davie Meiklejohn of Rangers took a free kick that Lambie was able to deflect, but Thomas Craig was there to place the bouncing ball neatly past Jackson. Lambie's efforts were great, but he wasn't as dominant as usual and Thistle were beaten 2-1. The remaining league matches in April saw Partick win two and lose three.

If losing the Scottish Cup Final to Rangers wasn't enough, Partick found themselves competing with them again in the Glasgow Charity Cup Final against Rangers on 3 May. Rangers would again win 2-1 with the 'sparkle and skill' they demonstrated at Hampden. Lambie was not in the line-up and Rangers' forward line took advantage with briskness and confidence. Partick's George Boardman scored his team's goal.

A summer break helped Thistle regroup. They met Aberdeen on 9 August in front of a crowd around 23,000 at Firhill Park, eager to get the season up and running. Partick forwards Torbet, Simpson and Ness used speed, intelligence and sharp counter attacks to threaten the Aberdeen defence. The Jags' own back line relied on the fine mobility of Lambie covering the penalty box, even while being harassed by opposition strikers. Jackson did a commendable job in goal and Thistle began the 1930/31 season with a win.

Saturday, 16 August brought Thistle back down to earth as they lost 2-0 to a depleted Kilmarnock reserve side at Rugby Park. Partick's Ness was shadowed for the whole 90 minutes and Thistle were disjointed. Only the deep midfield line of Lambie, the two wing-backs and goalkeeper Jackson were in decent form. Thistle then redeemed themselves with a 2-1 victory over Greenock Morton at Firhill Park. Both teams bolted out of the starting gate and fought with 'great zest'. Thistle had the better part of the match, and even though their forwards weren't at their best, they were smart enough in the penalty area when it mattered. Lambie was the 'best man' among the half-backs. Morton's front line had some good individual efforts but they were not enough to get the result.

The 6 September match against newly promoted East Fife proved to be a walk in the park for Thistle, who trounced their opponents 8-0. Inside the first 30 minutes the Jags had racked up six goals and benefited from mistakes from East Fife, who lacked speed, guile and competitive qualities. Taking full points at home with lots of goals was definitely welcome early in the season. Partick continued on a nice winning streak, seeing forward Simpson register 12 goals in 12 matches (including one hat-trick and four goals in one match). Lambie was absent for the month of October, although by mid-December Partick had racked up 12 wins, five losses and two draws.

Against Dundee on 15 December 1930, the veteran Lambie dominated the centre of the field. He won every high ball, and his long limbs seemed to spread all over the place. Lambie was a giant in defence as he held opponents at bay, but he also played a big part in attack when pressing up as an extra forward. He had one great shot and one great header in the first half, and there was no doubt he had the makings of a good leader.

Alex spent the best part of early 1931 off the field due to illness or injury and left Thistle at the end of his contract. He only managed 19 games over his final season with the club. In early September there were rumours that Alex had been offered a player-coach position at Fraserburgh. The *Hull Daily Mail* reported on 29 December 1931 that Alex had signed a contract for the remainder of the season at Swindon Town after a month-long trial with the club. On 20 February 1932 Alex gave a great performance against Bristol Rovers, being a tower of strength and holding up Rovers' forwards several times. On 28 March Lambie was solid against Exeter City, shadowing Childs, their midfield pivot. In a hard-fought match against Burnley, Lambie was the outstanding man on his side. He 'stayed with a plan', helping slow down the attacking waves and supporting his full-backs. On 31 May, the *Dundee Courier* reported that Lambie had extended his contract with Swindon and that he was the only Scotsman on the books.

Swindon suffered a 2-1 loss to Burnley in the FA Cup third round on 14 January 1933. After finishing the season with Swindon, Alex crossed the Irish Sea and signed with Distillery. The last public mention of his exploits on a football field came in the *Derry Journal* on 9 November 1936. The newspaper said he had played well against Derry City and could be useful at half-back. By late 1936, Distillery were third from the bottom of the Irish League table.

21st-Century Rugby Star

PATRICK LAMBIE emerged in 2009/10 as one of the finest rugby players in South Africa. Born on 17 October 1990 in Durban, South Africa, to Ian and Cathryn Lambie, Pat is the great-grandson of Alex Lambie. When Patrick's father, Ian, was born, he spent the first 12 years of his life in Troon with his Scottish parents: John (Jack) Lambie, who was born in Troon in 1924 and passed away in South Africa in 1997, and Neeta Buchanan, who continues to live in South Africa as of 2022.

Pat's parents are no strangers to rugby. Ian, who played as a winger or full-back with Natal (now the Sharks) in the 1980s, was also outstanding at school. His Natal career in the early 1980s ended prematurely through an injury that would be routine today. Pat's maternal grandfather, Nicholas Labuschagne, played as a hooker for England and the Barbarians. He won five caps for England between 1953 and 1955 while attending university. Born in Durban, South Africa, on 26 May 1931, Nicholas attended Hilton College in Natal and Cape Town University, before moving to England to study as a dental surgeon at Guy's Hospital. His debut for England came in January 1953 against Wales, but it was only in 1955 that he won the rest of his caps against Wales, Ireland, France and Scotland. Nicholas was a member of the team that won the 1955 Calcutta Cup. He later played for Western Province and Natal upon returning to South Africa.

An article in *Al Arabiya News* on 29 May 2011 detailed Nicholas's 80th birthday celebrations with his son, Nick, whose birthday falls on the same day as well. The article read, 'The Labuschagnes are remembered for many things, but they are remembered most of all for what they have given back to the society in which they flourished as businessmen, sportsmen, physicians, entrepreneurs, lawyers and philanthropists. A physician by training, a businessman by profession, and a rugby player and racing aficionado by vocation, Dr [Nicholas] Labuschagne is tall, distinguished and disarmingly genial. Dr Labuschagne, in his role as director of the national rugby authority, was the one who brought the 1995 World Cup to South Africa, which they won, and a victory that was featured in the film, *Invictus*.'

Early on in high school, Pat captained the rugby and cricket first teams at Michaelhouse, Pietermaritzburg. He was the leading points scorer in the 2009 under-21 Currie Cup and went on to make his senior debut for Natal later that same year against the Griquas. In 2010 Pat made his Super Rugby debut for the Sharks, scoring 25 of their 30 points in the Currie Cup Final against Western Province. Pat then played for the South Africa under-20 side at the IRB Junior World Championship in Argentina, earning a nomination for the IRB Junior Player of the Year award. That same year he made his Test debut for the Springboks versus Ireland in Dublin during the autumn internationals.

He was selected as the youngest member of the Springbok squad for the 2011 Rugby World Cup in New Zealand, where he started four of South Africa's five games. On 4 August 2010 Pat had been selected as the Currie Cup Player of the Month for July. He was also named South Africa's Young

Player of the Year in 2011. ESPN mentioned that Pat's 'first start for the Springboks had come after another hugely impressive Super Rugby campaign in which he broke the record for the most points scored by a Sharks player in one season'. In the 2012 issue of *GQ South Africa*, Pat said, 'I love playing rugby, I love the friendships, the memories, the travel and the different experiences overseas. I feel very blessed to be able to play the sport I love the most for a living.' He got married to Kate Symons on 18 January 2014.

In 2014 Lambie landed a 55-metre penalty in the final play of the Rugby Championship Test in front of 62,000 against New Zealand in Johannesburg. The conversion gave Springboks coach Heyneke Meyer his only victory over the All Blacks, and inflicted the world champions' first loss in almost two years.

Lambie was selected in South Africa's squad for the 2015 World Cup in England. He started their opening match, against Japan, as they suffered a shocking last-minute loss. Though Lambie was hardly to blame for the defeat, he was dropped from the starting squad against Samoa and wasn't involved against the USA. Pat came off the bench for all but one of the remaining six games, including the semi-final loss to New Zealand and the third-place play-off victory over Argentina, which marked his 50th Test appearance.

In December of 2015, Pat was selected as captain of the Sharks at fly-half. Sharks director of rugby Gary Gold stated, 'Pat's records and performances over the years speak volumes about the calibre of player he is. He is a natural born leader, who has shown on numerous occasions that he possesses all of the qualities needed to be a great captain, especially captaining a team he has supported all his life.' Pat was a versatile player who was effective at fly-half, inside centre and full-back with the Sharks.

Pat then suffered a concussion in the spring of 2016 and was ruled out of any league or international competition, including the Sharks' participation in the 2016 Super Rugby season. However, in June he was named as the Springboks' vice-captain, and in October he captained South Africa against the Barbarians during their autumn European tour.

Pat's older brother Nic (33 years) has just left the employment of Clifton College in Durban where he spent three years as a sports intern and then sports officer. Nic is now involved full time with a start-up business he has had an interest in for some four years. SportsCap is a software programme development company geared towards athlete and sporting code management and is gaining traction in the schooling and sporting federation fraternities.

Pat signed with the world-renowned Racing 92 in 2017, playing nearly 20 Top 14 and Champions Cup matches for the Parisian club. He announced his official retirement at the age of 28, on 19 January 2019, after a series of concussions. He was honoured by Racing 92 team-mates and staff in the dressing room on 2 March after the team's big victory over Stade Rochelais, with the presentation of a Racing 92 blazer and a well-crafted Racing 92 armchair. It was an emotional *merci* to Pat and his dedication to the team and the great sport of rugby. That same year, Pat and Kate welcomed their first child into the world.

Pat is enjoying life after rugby with a career in real estate blossoming in KZN with Collins Residential Developments. Pat is heading up sales at two premier residential estates on KZN's north coast, Zululami and Seaton.

He keeps in touch with rugby and helps out periodically at The Sharks with technical kicking and strategy skills. Pat and Kate are loving family life with their two sons, Jackson

(Jack) and Samuel (Sam) residing in Simbithi Eco Estate in Ballito. Jack is three years old, and Sam turns two in September, so they are keeping Pat and Kate busy!

Editor's Epilogue

THE STORY of the Browns, the Lambies, and all the other offshoots of this remarkable multi-generational sporting success story captures at once both sides of the nature/nurture debate. Is there such a thing as a born athlete? And how much does success in sport depend on the confluence of hard work and a heaped helping of luck?

There is no doubt that a family that can claim Hall of Fame careers as international-level athletes in multiple football codes can boast some semblance of genetic blessings passed down from generation to generation. From Alex Lambie and Jimmy Brown in association football in the early 1900s to the Springbok exploits of Pat Lambie a century later, this family's long track record at the top reaches of football in multiple guises makes a compelling case for some set of heritable traits that make them better on a pitch than the general population.

But the story of Jimmy Brown and his family also captures the contingencies that mark history in a way that shows how one's success in a sport can be nurtured in the right environment. When Jimmy took a chance on immigrating to the United States, it ultimately shaped his development as a soccer player and helped land him a spot on the 1930 US World Cup team. At the same time, World War Two adversely impacted both his own career and those of his two brothers. Contingencies give and contingencies take, and genetic blessings alone cannot guarantee success in the world of sport.

Where one is born and where one spends their formative years also seems to impact how one engages with sport and which football code earns the bulk of their attention. As a fun counterfactual to consider, we might imagine Peter Brown – whose contemporary John Gray said 'was a master at an overhead pass more associated with American football' – excelling as a quarterback on the gridiron had he been born on the opposite side of the Atlantic, or in another era, or even had made the same decision as his uncle and emigrated from Scotland to American shores.

What shines through more than anything in this family legacy is a passion for football in all its guises. For all the genetic advantages that the Browns, Lambies and the rest of the clan might enjoy, they collectively fostered an environment where those talents could be nurtured and maximised and instilled that passion to each new generation of progeny. In reading stories about times at the Brown family home in New Jersey, one can't help but imagine how *fun* it would have been to join everyone in the back yard for a kick-about. For as serious as each of these men might have been when a match was in progress or during their time on the touchline as coaches, they always seemed to remember that both soccer and rugby were first and foremost games to be enjoyed by their participants.

It was that same passion that drove James Brown to spend the past six years sleuthing through the life of his namesake grandfather and untangling the complex webs of his family's history in elite sport which spans three generations, three continents, and a pair of football codes. The same passion that James demonstrated in his high school playing days and onward into college and a semi-professional career on the pitch is just as evident in the preceding pages. Just as his father and mother were so instrumental to the preservation of American soccer history in the late 20th century, the work James has done and continues to do as a board member of the Society for American Soccer History follows in those footsteps.

I hope you as a reader have enjoyed hearing about the layers of the Brown family legacy and how that legacy has helped shape the histories of two sports on both sides of the Atlantic and on both sides of the equator. I certainly enjoyed working with James to frame this story and look forward to more detective work as he continues to dig into the hidden histories of football in all its guises.

Zach Bigalke
July 2022

Appendix A: Family Timeline

1908	James Brown junior born in Kilmarnock, Scotland
1915	John Brown born in Troon, Scotland
1919	Tom Brown born in Troon, Scotland
1920	James Brown senior moves to US
1921	Alex Lambie plays with Partick Thistle
1927	Alex Lambie wins Glasgow Merchants Charity Cup with Partick Thistle
1928	James Brown junior moves to US; Alex Lambie wins Dental Cup with Partick Thistle
1929–1930	James Brown plays amateur and professional soccer in US
1930	James Brown selected and capped four times with US national team for 1930 World Cup; wins bronze medal
1930 or 1931	James Brown and Mary Cormack marry (exact date unknown)
1931	Alex Lambie leaves Partick Thistle
1932–1934	James Brown plays for Manchester United; Alex Lambie joins Distillery in Ireland
1934	James Brown wins Manchester Senior Cup with United's reserves
1933	James Alexander Brown junior born in Manchester

1934–1936	James Brown plays for Brentford
1934/35	James Brown wins London Challenge Cup with Brentford's reserves
1935	George Brown born in Ealing, England
1936/37	James Brown plays for Tottenham Hotspur
1935–1942	John Brown plays for Clyde
1937–1940	James Brown plays for Guildford City
1937/38	James Brown wins Southern League championship at Guildford City; leading goalscorer
1938	John Brown capped twice for Scotland
1938/39	James Brown runner-up in Southern League at Guildford City; leading goalscorer
1938	Tom Brown plays for Ipswich Town
1938–1940	James Brown wins Surrey Combination Cup with Guildford City
1939	John Brown wins Scottish Cup with Clyde; James Brown wins Mayor of Aldershot Cup with Guildford City
1939	John (navy) and Tom (commandos) are drafted, and James is exempted from World War Two
1940/41	James Brown plays last season with brother John and ends career
1941	Peter (PC) Brown born in Troon, Scotland
1942–1944	John Brown plays for Hibernian
1944–1946	John Brown plays for Gillingham
1946–1948	John Brown plays for Hibernian
1947	Gordon L. Brown born in Troon, Scotland
1948/49	John Brown plays for Dundee
1948/49	James and Mary Brown move to the US
1948–1950	James Brown coaches varsity soccer at Greenwich High School

1948/49	John Brown ties for first place at footballers' and golfers' Daily Record Trophy in Cawdor, Scotland
1949/50	John Brown plays for and coaches Kilmarnock
1949–1952	George Brown plays soccer at Greenwich High School
1950–1952	James Brown creates Connecticut Soccer League and Greenport United; plays with George
1951/52	Tom Brown finishes career at Bury Town
1952–74	James Brown coaches Brunswick School varsity soccer and riflery
1953–1955	Nicholas Labuschagne plays rugby for England and the Barbarians; winning five caps for England and the 1955 Calcutta Cup
1953–1956	George Brown plays with German-Hungarians
1953	George Brown is MVP with German-Hungarians
1953–1956	George Brown wins three consecutive championships with the German-Hungarians
1956	George Brown is leading scorer and wins the New York State Cup with Elizabeth Polish Falcons
1956–1958	George Brown plays with Elizabeth Polish Falcons, father James coaches team
1957	George Brown selected and capped with US national team in World Cup qualifier in Mexico
1959	George Brown wins bronze medal at Pan-Am Games in Chicago
1962	John Brown wins the John Martin Golf Cup

1964–1976	Peter Brown plays rugby for West of Scotland and Gala, and captains Scotland
1969–1976	Gordon Brown plays rugby for Scotland
1971, '74, '77	Gordon Brown plays for the British & Irish Lions
1974	John Brown wins the Lord Ashton Golf Cup
1986	James Brown inducted into the US National Soccer Hall of Fame
1990	Patrick Lambie is born in Durban, South Africa
1995	George Brown inducted into the US National Soccer Hall of Fame
2000	James Brown inducted into the Connecticut State Hall of Fame; Tom Brown passes away
2001	Gordon Brown passes away and inducted into the International Rugby Hall of Fame
2005	James and George Brown inducted into the New England Soccer Hall of Fame
2005	John Brown passes away
2010	Gordon Brown inducted into the Scottish rugby Hall of Fame
2012	George Brown inducted into the Connecticut Soccer Hall of Fame
2015	*Glasgow Herald* selects the 50 greatest rugby players of all time: Gordon second and Peter 20th
2016	Pat Lambie captains South Africa's rugby team

Appendix B: Additional Recollections

Recollections about James Brown

'James Brown was an unusual signing for Manchester United, a Scot from Troon who was also an American. His uncle, Alex "Sanny" Lambie, was the former Partick Thistle centre-half and captain in the late 1920s.

'On his return to the UK in the 1932 close season after a few years of playing "soccer" in the USA, he became part of manager Scott Duncan's reconstruction project at the club after a few dismal seasons at Old Trafford. Signed in August 1932 by Duncan in the chief steward's room while still on the Anchor liner *Caledonia*, Brown was initially only on a month-long trial. He soon established himself with an uncanny way of pleasing the crowds by scoring directly from corners while United were battling in the Second Division, and became the second-highest scorer during his two seasons in Manchester. Midway through the following season, with United struggling, Brown became one of nine players on United's books that other clubs were invited to make offers for his transfer. He remained at Old Trafford until the end of the season before moving south to join Brentford in May 1934.

'These bare bones of his time at Old Trafford perhaps don't tell us too much about him. However, Brown had been "capped" by the United States while playing for a variety of teams in New York and New Jersey and played at the 1930 World Cup for his adopted country, scoring in their semi-final appearance.'

Mark Wylie, curator at Manchester United Football Club

'I am delighted to have been asked to write a testimonial for this sporting heritage book. Any football club with a long history will have players remembered long after they have hung up their boots. Old men and women will gather and recall those happy days of their youth when legendary players trod the turf of their favourite club. It's 100 years since the formation of Guildford City Football Club. Since 1921 there have been perhaps four or five players who truly could be considered "a legend" of the club. But arguably at the top of that list is Jim Brown.

'There will be very few people today who saw Jim play in the red and white stripes. Jim Brown was a goalscorer supreme and his period at the club between 1937 and 1940 coincided with Guildford's best ever side; a team that had World War Two not intervened may well have been elected to the Football League. Jim Brown made 150 appearances for Guildford City, scoring with his pace and shooting ability an incredible 148 goals. But there was far more to the man than three years spent in Guildford. Any man who scores in a World Cup semi-final, signs for Manchester United while on a transatlantic liner, and plays a part in the formation of the Players' Union is worthy of high acclaim.'

Barry Underwood MBE, secretary of Guildford City Football Club

Recollections about Jock Brown

'He was the loveliest guy you could meet and was old-school – very proper and correct. What a gem. At half-time in a match, I got a calf injury while playing at Murrayfield in Edinburgh, and he took proper care of me from every angle of the injury.'

Alastair McHarg, former Scotland international rugby union player, 1968–1979

'He was one of nature's gentlemen, the most modest of men, who let others talk admiringly of his illustrious soccer career. In the days when players had to make their own arrangements regarding medical treatment and when, even at international level, there was a cavalier approach to injury, having a qualified physiotherapist of Jock's calibre was a great luxury. He gave succour and encouragement to the team members and developed programmes for individual cases. Throughout my career I was plagued by hamstring problems, for which Jock devised a special series of exercises. A lovely man and an inspired appointment as Scotland's physio.'

Chris Rea, former Scotland international rugby union player, 1971

'My knowledge of PC's father was others' memories of visits to Jock's house for meals where you were quick to identify where PC and Gordon had obtained great handling skills – Jock when passing bottle items through the kitchen serving hatch, nothing was ever handed, and a bottle of sauce could appear at a rate of knots, and it was your job to catch it.'

John Gray, former rugby union player and coach for Gala and South of Scotland

'He was the ideal man to come into the Scottish national rugby team to care for their injuries. He was modest and loyal. He had a private room where he'd treat the players and whatever was talked about in the room stayed in the room. When asked what the players were talking about, Jock would say "this and that" every time. Jock was a real gentleman, and he had the largest hands. He had to be persuaded to talk about his playing days, and that attests to his modesty.'

Ian 'Mighty Mouse' McLauchlan, former Scotland international rugby union player, 1969–1979

'Uncle Jimmy was a real charmer. After Aunt Mary, George and Marilyn left for the States he would stop in at our house until he joined them, sometimes to eat, sometimes to stay over. Us kids would never eat the bread crust, but once he convinced us it would give us curly hair, so it was a fight to get the crust. He was hooked on dog racing. When his dog won, the whole family ate fish suppers and the dog slept in the big chair! We loved visiting Aunt Mary and him when we moved to the States, such a wonderful, thoughtful couple.'

Bill Brown, cousin and best friend of George Brown

Recollections about Peter Brown

'Peter always came across as quiet and reserved but he was a lot of fun and a great after-dinner speaker and always willing to do anything you asked of him. He was a great player and an amazing goal kicker. He'd dig his heel in the mud and build a tuft of mud, then he'd turn his back on the ball until he was ready to approach and nail the kick. He hit the ball side-footed (a yard wide was his foot!) and he very rarely missed.'

Jim Neilly, BBC radio and TV commentator

'Peter won his first cap in the second row as a 23-year-old in 1964. By the time I won my first cap in 1968, PC was out of favour with the selectors, and the Scottish captain was the feared and uncompromisingly blinkered Jim Telfer, who believed that the forwards did the hard graft and won the matches, and that the backs were there to look pretty, to tackle, to keep the pack going forward by kicking and to make up the numbers to 15. When PC was selected to replace him as both captain and number eight, it was a breath of fresh air. Through his force of personality and self-belief he released us from the straitjacket rugby of the Telfer era.

'The Scottish team of '71 played some of the most attractive, attacking rugby of any national side since the war, exemplified by the games against France in Paris, and what was described as the "Match of the Decade", against Wales at Murrayfield. Both were lost but both could and should have been won, and in both the Scots played with adventure and freedom instilled by the captain. By the time we played England in the Calcutta Cup at Twickenham and the following week in the centenary match at Murrayfield, the team had been moulded into a formidable force. PC can take much of the credit for that.

'He was, of course, a one-off character, a maverick and eccentric who never ceased to innovate and surprise. A seven-a-side genius in the great Gala side of the time, he would leap up and head the ball from the kick-off. He indulged in all manner of overhead passes, subtle kicks and gimmicks that could not be found in any instructional manual. The Calcutta Cup match at Twickenham, where the Scots had not won for 33 years, was Brown at his inspirational best. He delivered a passionate team talk before the match, and during it scored a try, delivered a long, looping scoring pass to your truly and duly kicked the conversion, later described by the legendary commentator Bill McLaren as going over the bar "like a wet haggis".

'A week later and England came up to Murrayfield for the centenary match when Scotland, playing an outrageous brand of running rugby, trounced their opponents by what was then a record margin, 26-6. As a side note, a special badge was created for that match which was worn by both sides and on which the English rose was intertwined with the Scottish thistle. Bill Dickinson, the recently appointed Scottish coach – or adviser to the captain as he was styled – delivered one of the shortest but most effective team talks in rugby history. "See that badge, lads? You know what happens when you grow a thistle alongside a rose? The thistle fucking strangles the rose, so go out and do the same to these English bastards!"

'There is no doubt in my mind that Peter was instrumental in changing the mindset of Scottish rugby and how it should be played. There was a terrific spirit within that Scottish side in 1971, engendered by PC's attacking instincts and self-belief, and as a by-product, he succeeded in banishing the inhibitions that had plagued the Scottish game in the 1950s and 1960s. The backs were the chief beneficiaries of that transformation and suddenly we were making openings and scoring tries. He himself missed out on selection for the 1971 British Lions tour of New Zealand, but the quality of the Scottish game that season meant that five members of the pack and two backs went on the tour.

'Peter had overwhelming self-belief. When he said before the '71 classic against Wales, "I'll get the better of Mervyn Davies [rated the best number eight in the world] at the tail of the line-out," he did just that. He believed it and he did it.'

Chris Rea, former Scotland international rugby union player, 1971

'I knew Peter especially well because of Gala and seven-a-side, over and above the international team. That team got to 26 out of 32 border finals and won Melrose three years in a row. Our team came to be known as the Magnificent Seven (well, in Gala at least). All seven had played for Scotland – Drew Gill, me, Arthur Brown, Dunky Paterson, PC Brown, Kenny Oliver and Johnny Brown, the last named representing his country's sevens team at Murrayfield.

'On the pitch, Peter was eccentric – if someone kicked off the ball towards him, Peter would be as likely to head the ball back into touch as he would be to catch it. He could catch a ball in mid-air with one hand. His body would bend four ways in every direction. Peter was spring-heeled.

'Peter talked about how his father would make him practise catching over and over, jumping and touching crossbars. My relationship with Peter revolved as much around rugby as it was intellectual. We talked about sports, golf and even poetry. Today, Peter still loves to recite poetry and is well-versed. He is so many things to so many people. Above all, however, he was a fantastic and I believe a much-underrated player. He remains and will always remain a close friend.'

John Frame, former Scotland international rugby union player, 1967–1973

'Peter was an accountant at the time, and very confident in his statistical analysis of the field of play and team-mates and opponents and was a very confident captain and player. Peter and I played in the second row together.

'During the 25th anniversary of the Scottish side beating England for the Calcutta, a player reunion was set, but I had booked a month-long trip to India and was one of the only players who didn't make it to the reunion. Peter commented, saying, "Typical McHarg, disappearing across to Calcutta because that's where he thought the reunion was taking place!"

'Peter gave the team confidence and helped give constructive criticism to encourage and lift up a player who might have been struggling. He was analytical and had a "balance sheet" showing how you ranked up against and higher than the opposition. Like an accountant, after all the analysis, Peter always showed how each Scottish player was better than his opposite man.'

Alastair McHarg, former Scotland international rugby union player, 1968–1979

'Peter [Marr College] and I [Ayr Academy] first played against each other on the school level. Sport was a big part of the curriculum in most schools back then. I don't remember having ever lost to Marr College and Peter said he'd probably only lost twice to Ayr Academy – a bit of gilding the lily [to pile excess on excess in a fun way] on both sides. We played each other twice a year during the college years, and then on a club level. Peter always turned out every Saturday because he loved playing club ball. Gordon wasn't much of a club player but more international, big-time player. He loved the crowds, huge stadiums and he wanted to start and star. Peter was eccentric with his moves in a game. His off-the-wall ideas often worked. People who saw Peter play seven-a-side rugby were able to see how well-rounded of a player he was. Tremendous hands, running, tackling and his eccentric kicking style that always made it over the ball.

'On the bus, Peter would often take out a pair of socks, roll them up into a ball and start juggling. On game night, Peter would head to bed early. As a captain, Peter had a different view of the game. He was straightforward – encouraging you to do your best.'

Ian 'Mighty Mouse' McLauchlan, former Scotland international rugby union player at loosehead prop, 1969–1979

'On the flipside of the coin when you talk about Peter, he was very different in his approach to forward play but extremely talented in his delivery in both second row and number eight play. When he arrived at Gala in the late 1980s, I found his methods in forward play a little extreme in that we could be rucking as a pack and he could be standing in the middle of the pitch with the three-quarters as he had already worked out, we were winning the ball and he would be more effective running with it.

'He was a master at an overhead pass, more associated with American football, and he could deliver a torpedo pass from a ruck won to the hands of an outside centre. In the modern game his skills would have been described as "brilliant". He was first and foremost a great rugby player who could entertain the crowd, and a great team-mate whose methods were a bit away from the norm and at the end of the day Peter is one of the greatest players Scotland ever produced. My son Richard still refer to when PC had been down at Netherdale coaching a junior or semi-junior team and he showed the young players how he could touch his fingers above the crossbar – that's some jump. He had amazing skills and as it was long before you could lift players in the line-out, I reckoned he could defy gravity and hover in the air till the ball was thrown to him.

'In the seven-a-side arena he was ahead of Gordon, and I was fortunate to play alongside him in a very successful Gala seven. In his first outing in a Gala seven at Earlston with Nat Carson and I in the forwards his warm-up caught us by surprise. Where Nat and I were used to doing a few limited stretches, PC proceeded to do a squat exercise with Arthur Brown over his shoulders.

'He was a great guy to have on your side, although he never knew what he was going to do next – it goes without saying if he did not know what he was going to do, it's obvious neither did the opposition. He was also the first forward ever that our supporters had seen head a ball into touch. If that was out of the norm then certainly his goal-kicking technique was as after lining the ball up he proceeded to turn his back on the ball, and walk a few steps, turn round to face the ball, wipe his nose on the sleeve of his jersey and bang, over it would go. When the club signed a jersey sponsorship with Adidas much to the dissatisfaction of the SRU, the Border supporters in humour suggested that we had signed the deal so that we could all have three stripes on our jersey like the result that the nose wipe was having on PC's jersey.

'It has to be said that even the flight of PC's kicks was not that elegant, and I am sure it was the great Bill McLaren who described a successful kick at Twickenham as "that ball's flight over the bar looked like an unwrapping fish supper".

A thing that always amazed me about PC was, when in his suit of clothing he looked big, but in a rugby strip he look much bigger. He had a presence and his handling, passing, tackling, and kicking ability was amazing.

'At the outset I was a little quizzical of his approach, and after one or two games I was asked by the selectors, "Well what do you think of the big guy?" "As an individual great but you could not afford to have eight of him in the same pack," to which the selectors' response was, "Give me eight of his type any day." When I think back maybe my assessment was based on, if we could find eight like him I was out. Those were my initial thoughts but after packing down in the second row with him that season, I was seeing brilliance that already had I think eight or nine Scottish caps.

'PC's talents were most eloquently described by Norman Mair, rugby writer for *The Scotsman*, who wrote, "But when his eye is in, he is capable of banging over goals with any of them, while simultaneously causing much hasty revision of the laws of ballistics. Blessed with a sense of position exclusively his own, marvellously adhesive hands, and a punt with either foot, nonetheless parabolic delivery of ball on to foot. Peter Brown has a deceptively disjointed action that yet cannot hide the co-ordination of a born ball-player." I consider myself lucky to have played alongside the great PC Brown.'

John Gray, former rugby union player and coach for Gala and South of Scotland

Recollections about Gordon Brown

'I knew Gordon from an opponent's perspective. He was a great guy with a great attitude blessed with a nature that you never would have thought would respond to a member of the "boiler house" brigade in the second row, but he certainly did. Gordon was very much a standard textbook second row, a highly competitive jumper, natural strength to be a first-class asset to have in any scrum and made great tackles when needed.

'My experience with Gordon was of a very competitive nature as I was given the job to mark him in the line-out, which was a joke – as I could hardly reach his armpit far less out-jump him. My first introduction to Gordon was when PC had him as a visitor to his home in Galashiels and it just so happened that the late Dunc Paterson (if my memory serves me correctly, I think Dunc and Gordon got their first cap together against SA in 1969) and I had arranged an early-season Saturday training session and young Gordon Brown joined us at Netherdale. In the bar after I was asked what I thought about PC's brother to which I responded, "Well he is not a PC." He was young and "raw" but as he progressed in the sport, he was to achieve greatness and selection for three Lions tours certainly proved that. Gordon as I already highlighted was a very orthodox second row forward very unlike his brother PC who definitely "stepped outside the box" and Gordon was never a sevens forward of the quality of his brother.'

John Gray, former rugby union player and coach for Gala RFC and South of Scotland

'He was the ultimate baby-faced assassin. A smile that would melt hearts and the life and soul of any party with the most infectious laugh – usually at his own jokes! But on the field, he was transformed. Hard as teak with a ferocious will to win, he never took a backward step. He was, like Peter, a man for the big stage, and the bigger the occasion the better he played. If he wasn't always firing on all cylinders, week in week out for his club West of Scotland, he never once let the side down, but always entered the international arena in peak condition.

'Coming into the Scottish side for Peter Stagg, at 6ft 10in, the tallest man ever to have played international rugby, Gordon at 6ft 5in and 16st, brought a better balance along with ballast to the second row, alongside Alastair McHarg. For such a big man he had enviable athletic skills which he put to great use around the field, but it was his work in the tight which helped transform Scottish forward play.

'My favourite "Broon frae Troon" story concerns our post-playing days when we commentated together at the 1995 Rugby World Cup in South Africa. The match was Scotland against Tonga. The Tongans are delightful people but pronouncing their names is a commentator's nightmare, and on this occasion, there was a particular problem with the Tongan tighthead prop who rejoiced under the name of Fuko Fuka. Ten minutes into the game, and Fuko Fuka, in full view of the TV cameras, took a swipe at the Scottish full-back Gavin Hastings, knocking him out in the process. Skilfully I avoided the banana skin by giving the hospital pass to my co-commentator, "Looks like the Tongan tighthead is in serious trouble here Gordon." There was a pause before the never-to-be forgotten reply, "Aye, silly Fuka!"

'Gordon, for his part, brought stability and muscular aggression to the Scottish pack. In the 1971 Calcutta Cup match and up against the almost psychopathic brute force of Nigel Horton, Gordon came out on top with the result that the English selectors dropped their most formidable forward for the centenary match the following week.'

Chris Rea, former Scotland international rugby union player, 1971

'That 1974 team was the greatest pack in Lions history. Gordon was an important part of it. He was a big boy and was a very good player at that level. With the Lions you're away for three months and training every day. Gordon won three tours and that was an exceptional feat. Gordon was always a first choice for the Test side.

'Gordon brought discipline, for great with his team-mates as a motivator, and did everything he was asked to – the best he could. He was a second row forward – scrummage and line-out forward. He played with the best against the best. During the 1974 tour, Gordon was interviewed by phone and asked what he'd like to do while he was there – shoot a lion or whatever, and he said no, "I just want to play golf with the famous Gary Player." A few days later he got a call from Gary who said, "Get two of your mates and we'll play a four-ball," so they played together and then Gary invited Gordon and his mates back to his home for dinner.'

Syd Millar, 1974 British & Irish Lions coach

'In 1969 Gordon was working for the British Linen Bank in Ayr. In that summer, I worked in the Butlin's holiday camp in the kitchen and then transferred over to being a plain-clothed security man. The British Linen Bank had a branch in the reception area of the camp and regulations required that someone from security needed to be there from 10am to 1pm every day of the week. Ernie Nash, Gordon's physical education teacher, told me that a guy was gonna be at the camp all summer and was hoping to head out on tour with Scotland to Argentina. Ernie said, "You've seen Peter

Brown playing, haven't ya?" I said, "Yes I have," and Ernie replies, "This is Peter's younger brother, Gordon." I asked if he was as good as Peter. Ernie replied, "He's better and he's a lovely guy!"

'So the following Monday, I pitched up and there was Broony, this big baby-faced monster, he was huge, who'd probably never shaved a day in his life, and they saw each other every day and became great buddies. At the end of July the same summer, Gordon invited me to the Highland Games in Ayr at Dam Park and to participate in the tug-of-war competition on his side, the West of Scotland team consisting of the great Sandy Carmichael [50 caps for Scotland over 11 years], Quintin Dunlop [hooker for Scotland], Alec Wilson. Needless to say, with all that heavy artillery, we won the tug-of-war competition! We also had a 4x100m relay race and Gordon ran the third leg and accelerated past everyone – he could run. [Player not remembered], then Chris Rea [Scotland and the British & Irish Lions in 1971] and Dave Sheddan who was like a greyhound and a sprinter. They won the race by a mile! Gordon went off to Argentina, although he wasn't capped until the following December against South Africa.

'We always kept in touch and Gordon would always send postcards from wherever he was. I went on to teach in 1977 and went into broadcasting just as Gordon stopped playing. We crossed paths often as we did charities together and Gordon was doing a lot of after-dinner speaking engagements and stayed friends forever. Gordon did some TV commentating with me and Ian "Mighty Mouse" McLauchlan, Chris Rea and Ian Robertson as well. At that time, Gordon decided to leave the building society where he had worked and devote his time to after-dinner speaking because he was making money hand over fist and then a short while later he was diagnosed with cancer.

'One particular lunch he was speaking at Northampton and had to break away because he had to take the train to Bath or Exeter to do a dinner, and he brought a Rangers football to auction off. He was sitting in a compartment and halfway through the trip he had forgotten to get the ball signed by the Rangers players. Luckily, he had a sheet with the list of players and signatures, so he got a pen and forged the signatures on the ball. He finished the signatures and put the ball back in the plastic bag and settled in. A guy across the way, reading the newspaper, interrupted him and asked if he was Gordon Brown, and he said "aye aye" and the guy said he was going to the same dinner and asked if Gordon would be terribly offended if he didn't put a bid in for the "authentically signed" Rangers ball that Gordon just finished signing! After a long laugh, Gordon said, "No, I don't mind if you don't tell anyone," and the men shared a chuckle.

'A fond memory about Gordon and Bill Beaumont before a match (Bill came on as a replacement), Gordon grabbed Bill and said, "If you don't keep up with me, I'm gonna kick your arse up and down the pitch!" Welcome to the Lions! When England finished at the bottom of the Five Nations tournament way back when, they received a wooden spoon for finishing last and they decided that they might as well celebrate the fact that we're hopeless! So we founded this Wooden Spoon Society and organised luncheons and days out and all the money raised went to children.'

Jim Neilly, BBC radio and TV commentator

Very amiable men – all the Browns. Jock was the rubs man, known as Jock Brown. Very good masseur. At the Sportsman's Charity dinners, which I ran from 1983 to 2010, I used Gordon both as a brilliant speaker and an equally awesome auctioneer from the mid-1980s to 2000, along with his great pal, Fergus Slattery, on the Ireland Murrayfield matches. It always took place on the eve of the Ireland v Scotland or Calcutta England v Scotland game; 500-plus attended and £85,000 would be raised. Gordon spoke twice. Superb after-dinner speaker. Gordon would always stay with me and my family.

'After those auctions, at our home, a nice bottle of malt whisky would be assaulted through to the wee hours as we'd put the world to rights. During one Christmas holiday visit me and his wife, Gordon and Linda all went to a church and Gordon told me, "This will be the greatest Christmas of my life, this is when I'll beat cancer!" because Gordon was scheduled to have a bone marrow transplant.

'One of my lasting memories was of an emotional tribute fundraising dinner in London before his passing, where over 1,200 people came to honour Gordon, including Johan de Bruyn from South Africa, he of the glass eye story. On his last appearance at the Sportsman's Charity dinner, Gordon said to me earlier that he'd be late and after I asked why, Gordon mentioned he agreed to speak at a lunch in Dublin for his mate Fergus Slattery. So after all the guests had arrived at the dinner, I got up and explained that Gordon would be late – but I reminded everyone that Gordon would surely try and slip in the side entrance and have a seat without being noticed. I alerted the man at the far end of the room to let him know when Gordon made his way in. And as right as rain, Gordon did just that, tried to sneak in without notice. The full house stood up and gave a long round of applause and there was such emotion that filled the room and that was Gordon Brown, just an amazing man and I loved him. Gordon was part of the furniture, part of the family. He was a brother.'

John Frame, former Scotland international rugby union player, 1967–1973

'I was first introduced to rugby in school by a man called Mr Murray, "Stacher", because he had a fancy moustache. He started the school rugby team in a football-dominant county, and I would go watch my brother play. One day, the team was a player short, and they saw my size and asked if I wanted to play. So, I suited up and played in the back, even though I had never played a minute of rugby in my life! Two years later, at Irvine Academy, Mr Murray was in the gym asking kids what they played. Murray, "What's your name?" Answer, "Smith." Murray, "Do you play football?" Answer, "Aye." [To the next boy, and so on.] Murray, "What's your name?" Answer, "[Alastair] McHarg." Murray, "You've got a brother, John?" Answer, "Aye." Murray, "You play rugby! No choice!" And that was history. Irvine Academy played against Marr College. Later on, Gordon and I were on the national squad tours and would travel together, even sharing a room for seven years. I often do after-dinner speaking engagements, but free of charge, for friends and associates.

'After moving close to London, I worked as a draftsman and attended night school. Later, I moved to Devon and would commute for four or five hours each way to play rugby for London Scottish which was amateur status at the time. Sometimes I had to take three days off at a time for international matches. The Scottish Rugby Union was not keen on turning professional back then and money was tight. Also, there was no official "coach" but an "advisor to the captain". Players had to pay for the whole kit themselves. Jerseys were like gold dust at the time and cost about five guineas.

'An example of tight federation pockets back in those days, I recall when myself and a team-mate had to face severe weather conditions in the south of London to make our way up to London by taxi to get a train for Edinburgh. We sent in our expense notes and a letter came back from the SRU secretary that said, "In the late 1880s, Jock McTavish, from Edinburgh station, took a horse-drawn cab to the stadium and charged two pence for the fare. Had he taken a tram to the match it would have cost one pence, so one pence was deducted from the expense notes." The same logic was applied to their journey through knee-high snowfall to make it to the match.

'After my playing days were over, I moved into purchasing agricultural machinery and was a purchasing director which required a large amount of travel worldwide, like Turkey, India, and China.

'Scotland toured in Argentina in 1969 during very difficult times, running around the pitch looking out not to get punched by the opposition. Gordon was in a mini stand, just going ballistic because of the favouritism and unruliness. Gordon always promoted himself in fun ways; for example, meeting with the press he always had a silly hat on to get in the papers and it was always good-natured. I played a loose type of game, and my mind was preset to do certain things and always running about, whereas Gordon was getting into the more nitty-gritty dealings and digging his heels in the scrums. It was a good blend of team-mates for the Scotland team at that time. Very complementary. At the 2001 ceremony dinner honouring Gordon, I asked Broony if we could get a photo of the way we were in the second row. We put our arms around each other, took a photo and I said to Gordon, "Hey Broony, isn't this great!" Gordon was a massive force in rugby. It was a privilege for me to play with him and share a room.

'Gordon's eight tries in South Africa; helping to build up the Famous Front Five; 1971 Scotland v England photo where I'm looking at Peter and Gordon, arms around each other as they approached me after the match – that's what Gordon and Peter gave to rugby, but it was also the Ayrshire connection. The relief that we beat England. I still feel that pride and honour. So many teams before had been so close to doing the same as they did in 1971, but we were the ones. The last time Scotland beat England was in 1938 on that level.

'Winning for your country is a historic achievement. Ayrshire, not having the deep foundations and history in rugby, has been greatly represented on the national and British Lions touring side. Having brothers for the same side competing on the highest levels and honours on the Scottish national side representing Scotland and the British & Irish Lions throughout the world, with Jock always in the wings as a mentor to all, Peter and Gordon have left a great legacy. A unique team or Cinderella Men from Ayrshire. During the period of competing at a high level and being an amateur at the same time was a great achievement.'

Alastair McHarg, former Scotland international rugby union player, 1968–1979

'Gordon would come late into the club season and play just enough games to get fit for the internationals and tours. He would excel in the big-time international games. We used to think that Gordon could hear a photographer's camera clicking a mile away.

'Gordon was a great "tourist". Being on tour for three months at a time, Gordon was forced to train every day and would be at his best. Being in constant rugby company with his mates created strong bonds, especially the 1971 and 1974 tours. Gordon was quieter and social at the same time. He'd often hang with the fellas until late at night.

'When Gordon passed away in 2001, there was a huge outpouring of honest affection and he was dearly loved and sorely missed. He wasn't an after-dinner speaker, he was a showman. Gordon knew how to work a crowd and win them over. At one of the Wooden Spoon Society dinners one year, Ian and Gordon arrived with Gordon dressed in a kilt and the lady welcoming them asked Ian to come with her to a VIP room and Gordon was sent to another room. After a time apart, Ian went back to the lady and asked if she knew who the guy in the kilt was, and she said, "I think he's the piper," and Ian said, "He's tonight's speaker!" Of course, she was embarrassed and went to say how sorry she was. Of course, Gordon took the mickey out of her for the rest of the evening.'

Ian 'Mighty Mouse' McLauchlan, former Scotland international rugby union player, 1969–1979

Recollections about George Brown

'First and foremost, your parents were lovely. I came from Jersey City and didn't come to the HOF [Hall of Fame] because of my soccer background, but my museum background. My fondness of your mother and father was that they were very kind and gave me the time necessary. Others might have been critical, and they looked at it as me being a part of the team. You were on a team, and they wanted to make their team-mates better and the team better as a whole. Peg was always in the archives or just around for day-to-day and operational at the HOF. George was there for the long-term relationships and the vision or direction of the HOF. It really helped me. I remember spending time with George. He shared insights about the history of the HOF, certain HOFamers, and was supportive about getting me out in the community, like the local Rotary Club in Oneonta.

'When the financial crisis hit in 2008, it was obvious that there would not be any more investments in the HOF. There was a political dynamic within the governance of the HOF, because of the strong local focus – investment of time and funds, in making the HOF possible. Economic development was first and foremost. Your father was different, an anomaly, as he had a strong legacy in the sport and was local at the same time. They were devotees to the HOF and the sport. They were not involved in the local and national tensions centred around the sport – for example, like the location of the HOF for attracting more visitors and have bigger inductions. Time, energy and emotion sums up the efforts at the HOF.

'When Mia Hamm was to be inducted, do we have the ceremony in Oneonta, Giants Stadium, the Rose Bowl, for example. Those were questions and realities the HOF had to confront. Personally, I most enjoyed seeing the kids playing in the local tournaments and in the museum. That's what it's all about. That little field in the museum was great. Of course, the inductions were great to honour those placed in the HOF, receiving their jacket, heading to the podium, and listening to their speeches, but having a venue where you can learn more about soccer's history and looking towards the future. I was there for a short time and many others had been there for a long time, wanting to do good and the outcome was tough. There were many wonderful and magical things that happened at the HOF.'

Jonathan Ullman, former president and chief operating officer of the National Soccer Hall of Fame, 2007–2010

'I recall the rumours swirling at the beginning of the 1993 soccer season. Cabot High School is located in a remote region in the north of Cape Breton Island, and at the time would have had around 300 students from grades seven to 12. Historically what school sports teams there were had to make do with whatever coaches were available, most often schoolteachers or community members. The word on the street was that this year the girls' soccer team was going to have a "real" coach: some retired Scottish-American guy who had recently moved to the area and had apparently played on the US national soccer team and coached teenage boys in the US at a high level.

'I recall my first impressions of him and thinking how American he seemed: a bit loud and brash by Canadian standards, and he was insistent that we call him "Coach". For a group of girls who were used to referring to even their school teachers by their first name this was a big change. Who the hell did this guy think he was? And I wonder what his first impressions were of us. Instead of a team of super-committed elite-level players who lived and breathed soccer and trained in their spare time, I'm sure a significant proportion of our team members (including me) weren't even comfortable with basics such as the offside rule. Instead of the team being selected from a large pool of potential players, essentially anyone who showed up to practice was on the team, including multiple sets of siblings and of course cousins as well. To say he had his work cut out for him is an understatement.

'But over the course of our short season he quickly brought a new order to our group. He drilled us in the basics during our twice-weekly practices and did an amazing job of teaching us team strategy: we were to use a "diagonal defence" strategy to shut down attacks from the opposing team, and the rule for the forwards was, "You can't score if you don't shoot, so as soon as you can smell the goal: SHOOT!" We also had to always keep our shirts tucked in, have our socks pulled up over our shin guards, never trash talk the other team, and only the captains were permitted to speak with the referee. There were a lot of new rules to follow.

'And would you believe it, in his very first season with us, "Coach" led our obscure team all the way to the final of the Nova Scotia Provincial Championships. During the game we religiously followed the diagonal defence strategy to shut down the other team and our forwards shot at the first opportunity: we went on to win the final 5-3. I recall feeling disbelief when the final whistle blew: had that just really happened? We were all screaming with excitement as only teenage girls can do, and he was right in the middle of the celebrations with us, grinning from ear to ear and hugging each and every one of us.'

Heather Murray, defender and co-captain of the Cabot girls' soccer team, 1993–1996

'When I think of his accomplishments on the field, in business, advice on any subject, his friendship and the wonderful family that he and Peggy raised, I am not ashamed to say he is still my hero. George came to Scotland in 1957 to try out for the famous Glasgow Celtic. He did not make the team but the newspapers loved "The Yank at Parkhead". My hero! His main buddy in the group was Jim Sharkey. The team took care of his accommodation, but he still managed to come visit us, one time bringing a carload of team-mates. Just imagine a young teenager seeing all those famous players in his house, even though I wore a red, white, and blue scarf! Only my hero.

'One time he tried to improve his horrible golf swing in our living room and only succeeded in destroying the overhead lights! But that was excusable, he was loveable George, so popular. Around 2008 we were both invited to the Rochester Rhinos v New England Revolution game, George to do the ceremonial kick-off in his Hall of Fame jacket and me as a guest because George "volunteered" me to make the winning team nameplates for the Dewar Trophy.'

Bill Brown, cousin and best friend

Recollections about Dave Brown

'Some of my most cherished memories are growing up with the Brown family. Yes, soccer was a big part of that, but there was so much more.

'But let's start with soccer. Meeting Dave in junior high school, after he and his family moved from Houston to New Jersey, I was introduced not only to soccer, but to my lifelong best friend. We played soccer 24/7. Except for school nights, we would sleep over at one house or the other – wherever we landed that day. The next morning the first question was, "What do you want to do?" The answer was always, "Let's kick a ball around." And this usually lasted most of the day. Back yard, in the pool, against the fence, in the house or running down the neighbourhood streets, one guy on each side, passing it to one another, trying to place it between cars and exactly at the foot of the other guy running at pace.

'There were countless back yard soccer games – with Dave, his father George, his brother Jim, and occasionally his grandfather Jim Brown senior. And any number of other friends who happened to be around at the time. Both George and Jim Brown senior were World Cup players, so we learned from the best. Some technique, but mostly how to have fun. And cheat like hell.

'At family gatherings, I remember when Jim Brown senior would call Dave and I over to tell us a story, and the stories were always great. But for some strange reason, he was not able to tell stories without Scotch. So he'd start by saying, in his wonderful Scottish accent, "Davey, Danny, get me a Scotch, but don't tell your grandmother."

'One day we were in the pool with Dave – probably one outside the pool kicking a ball at the other one playing goalkeeper in the pool – when George Brown came home and parked in the garage, which was on the far side of the pool, the side opposite the house, thus requiring you to walk around the pool to get from the garage to the house. This must have been a particularly long day for George, since he, in full suit with briefcase, walked from the garage to the pool, directly into the pool, across the pool, up the ladder and into the house, straight-faced, never saying a word. I can't help but hear the song words "so you had a bad day" in my head. George always had such a great sense of humour. A standard joke as his hair became grey was, "No, it's not grey, it's blond." Years later, my hair is now mostly blond".

'Dave and I both played varsity soccer in our senior year, but he was a far better and more experienced player than I was. I loved the game, and still do, having played adult rec [recreational] soccer for years, on and off, and coaching my kids. But Dave was clearly a level above. I remember playing with many other great guys, and good friends, that year too: Anthony DePalma, Bill Kraus, Curtis Lightburn, Brendan Quinn, Bill Elston, and many more.

'Dave and I both played club soccer at Farcher's Grove too, which was quite an experience. Farcher's Grove was a bar with a soccer field on the side. Our locker room was in the back of the bar and I remember a sign as you walked into the bar which said "no cleats in the bar". You can imagine how "spirited" games were with parents, beers in hand, sitting in the bleachers next to the field. Parents are loud and obnoxious enough when sober.

'I'll end my walk down memory lane with a more touching memory. At Dave's wedding, George, Jim senior, Jim, Dave and I wore kilts. It was November in New Jersey, so there was a bit of a George Costanza moment, but I digress. Dave's grandfather, Jim senior, was in poor health, in a wheelchair and on oxygen. I recall Dave and I carrying his wheelchair up the stairs to the second floor where the ceremony was held. I believe that was the last time I saw Jim senior. But I remember him smiling from ear to ear.

'Soccer was the foundation of many priceless memories growing up with the Brown family.'

Dan Smith, Scotch Plains-Fanwood High School class of 1983

'I have fond memories of the Brown family from growing up in Scotch Plains-Fanwood in the late 1970s to early 1980s. I believe the Scotch Plains-Fanwood Soccer Association was founded in 1977, and our fathers were among the pioneers and early architects of the programme. At the outset, my father Bob coached a neighbourhood rec team called the Rowdies with Tom Pauly, Mike Reilly, David Read and Kevin Haggerty among my team-mates. Jack Quinn led the Gunners with Brendan and Brian Quinn, Terry Christie, Connie Gentile and Anthony DePalma. The teams from the [Terrill Junior High School] south side of Scotch Plains were the Timbers and maybe the Sounders. I recall Mr Elston being a coach. Anyway, I presume your father George and brother Dave were aligned with one of these early teams.

'Another early memory was your father as lead referee instructor. I believe we had some classroom-type sessions at your house, and others in the community meeting room at the Fanwood train station. Your father must have had a lot of patience teaching the Laws of the Game to a bunch of American kids that had barely seen or played the sport before.

'My next set of memories is senior year of high school in 1982/83. Back in those days underclassmen got very little playing time on the varsity. It was mostly seniors that played. Probably because we were largely a bunch of athletes that had only been playing soccer for five or seven years and weren't really true soccer players yet. So the older, stronger, faster, more athletic upperclassmen commanded the most playing time. So it wasn't until senior year when Dave and I could really shine. We were playing a 4-3-3 and up the middle of the field was Danny Difrancesco at striker, Dave at central midfielder, me at stopper, Curtis Lightburn at sweeper and Brendan Quinn as goalkeeper.

'In hindsight, Dave was a bit ahead of our time. He was a finesse player. He had a wonderful first touch and ball skills and played some brilliant balls that the rest of us were often unable to visualise in the game at that time. And he had this great head of curly hair that would flow like his style of play.

'He could also be very scrappy. I recall him launching into slide tackles with a long, outstretched leg that just seemed to be able to poke the ball away. Although not a big guy, he was indeed a fighter. And a team player. Somehow, I would come forward from the back and take a bunch of the free kicks and penalties, and I don't recall Dave ever putting up a fuss about it.'

Bill Krauss, Scotch Plains-Fanwood High School class of 1983

'One thing I remember about Dave's grandfather was having him watch a game when we were probably about 13 or 14 and after having played the ball out of the back unsuccessfully at one point, he pulled me aside at half-time and said, "Just kick the ball as far up the field as you can, lad."

'As for Dave himself, I remember him being a skilled player on a high school team full of hooligans. I remember playing with him after college as well when we both played for the Italian American club in Scotch Plains. He had previously been playing in the Portuguese league in Newark and said that after his game one day somebody went to his car, pulled out a gun and started shooting at the ref. He said the guy told him he wasn't trying to kill him, he was just trying to scare him. Dave said, "OK, thanks, I'm done here." My last soccer interaction with Dave was some time ago when our daughters played against each other when they were in middle school. Dave was the same mellow guy he always was, just watching the game and loving it.'

Brendan Quinn, Scotch Plains-Fanwood High School, class of 1983

'Dave and I would talk about soccer and playing under Brez [Tom Breznitsky], what we thought the starting line-ups should be while we were drawing circles and shapes on drafting paper (we would laugh about it all the time as we felt we were back in first grade). We played together in town leagues and for the high school team. Dave was one of the better technical players on our team and we would practise one on one sometimes at the high school or if I remember correctly at Terrill Middle School. I also remember when we took the referee class and received our patches after the class was over and actually made pretty good money for a few hours on Saturdays reffing games. I remember many good memories with Dave and I think about all of my high school buddies from time to time.'

Danny Difrancesco, Scotch Plains-Fanwood High School 1980–1982

'David was one calm, cool and quiet player. Ahead of his time from a technical standpoint.'

Scott Wustefeld, Scotch Plains-Fanwood High School class of 1984

'What a happy coincidence it was to connect with the Brown family growing up in Fanwood, NJ. Early on in 1980, I took a referee certification course run by the Scotch Plains-Fanwood

Soccer Association. Our class met for several evenings in an upstairs room in the Fanwood Train Station, but little did we know that our instructor was a US soccer legend by the name of George Brown. George always seemed very happy during the classes, and it was like his face couldn't do anything else but smile.

'A few years later, we got to know George's oldest son, David Brown, while playing for Scotch Plains-Fanwood High School. David was a talented midfielder that came into his own during his senior season. David was a leader on the field and was instrumental in that team's run to the finals of the Union County Tournament in the fall of 1982. At David's high school graduation party, I was fortunate enough to meet his famous grandfather Jim Brown, who we later learned played for Manchester United and scored for the United States in the semi-finals of the 1930 World Cup in Uruguay. Quite a soccer bloodline!

'After starting my career in coaching college soccer in the late '80s, my very first "home visit" to a recruit's home was at the Browns' house to recruit David's younger brother Jim. Jim was a solid player that we felt would be a good addition to the Southern Connecticut programme in the build-up to the early National Championship years. Sadly, we didn't land him and someone else benefited from Jim's talents.

'Soon after arriving as coach at the University of Bridgeport in 2000, I was surprised to learn that among the many proud soccer alumni was my former referee instructor from Fanwood. It was great fun reconnecting with George after those many years. By then, George had settled in Oneonta with Mrs Brown (or Peggy as George called her) and was now involved with running the National Soccer Hall of Fame, of which both George and his dad, Jim, were both inductees.

'We spoke on the phone from time to time and caught up on life, and he filled me in on what David and Jim were up to. I later learned that George was close friends with our Connecticut's own local National Soccer Hall of Famer, Chico Chacurian, who was on my coaching staff.

'It always struck me as a little odd how my path kept crossing with the Brown family, but I'm so glad that it did. George Brown, having been such an accomplished player (from such a legendary soccer clan), was a wonderful gentleman that continued to give back to the game he loved so dearly. Now as a coach, I continue to be grateful for the insight into the referee's mind that George provided all of our eager young soccer brains back in Fanwood all those years ago.'

Brian Quinn, Scotch Plains-Fanwood High School class of 1982

'I knew the Brown family early in my soccer career as I had the pleasure of being coached by Dave and Jim's father during my years playing inter-city. It was not until high school that I started playing with Dave on the same field. The things that always impressed me about his game were not only his soccer brain but his vision, technical skill level and the relentless engine that he possessed. I modelled a lot of my game after him and always watched how he reacted to various scenarios.

'His senior year he was given the Johan Neeskens Award as being the most complete player on the team that year and I always thought that was fitting for him. He played his club ball for Farcher's and then went on to play at Drew University. During my high school senior year I remember Coach Brez taking me to watch Dave play for Drew and Bill Elston for Moravian. Nothing had changed, Dave controlled the midfield with the same intensity I had remembered from high school. It was a pleasure playing with him and he is fondly remembered as one of the true "soccer" players out of the storied Scotch Plains-Fanwood varsity soccer programme.'

Michael Webb, Scotch Plains-Fanwood High School class of 1984

Recollections about Jim Brown

'I thought it was simply a friendly soccer game in the back yard of a friend's house on a beautiful Saturday morning after a cook-out. I was completely wrong! I should have known something was different when everyone who was playing began taking off their shoes and socks. I have played soccer of course for years, but always with my shoes on. This new game called "barefoot soccer" was a sort of introduction to the intensity of soccer in the Brown household. As a young, impressionable high school student at the time, I did not understand how serious these back yard games were in this family of soccer legends, until this Saturday afternoon.

'I met the youngest of the Brown family, James Brown in seventh grade, but did not fully become an "adopted" member of this family until the elder Brown, George, could see how my toes held up in that inaugural game in their back yard. Although I remember the game was enjoyable, at some point my body went one way and my big toe on my right foot went another. I tore a tendon in my toe, an injury which would remind me for years to come. The Brown family played the beautiful game at another level, whether in the back yard, on the street, in a park, or in a stadium, this game was truly a family affair.

'Any time I would be with Jim, we always had a soccer ball. We might be in the parking lot of the train station, passing, dribbling, or juggling, always improving our touch. My skill as a soccer player was directly connected to my relationship with the Brown family. It would not be until many years later I would be able to fully appreciate being around this family and hearing the stories of how deep and historic soccer was in their bloodlines.'

Paul Pace, Scotch Plains-Fanwood High School class of 1990